HOW
SUCC
IN
A LEVELS

HOW TO SUCCEED IN A LEVELS

Second Edition

HOWARD BARLOW

KOGAN
PAGE

To Mary, Araminta, Leander and Douglas

'Read not to contradict or confute,
Nor to believe and take for granted,
But to weigh and consider.'

'To extend awareness of your own
Needs, expectations, feelings,
From which will flow your own
Conclusions, goals, actions.'

'It is for you to decide.'

First published in Great Britain in 1985 by
Kogan Page Limited, 120 Pentonville Road,
London N1 9JN
Second Edition 1988

British Library Cataloguing in Publication Data

Barlow, Howard, *1945–*
    How to succeed in A levels. — 2nd ed.
    1. England. Secondary schools. G.C.E.
    (A level) examinations. Techniques.
    Manuals.
    I. Title
    373.12'62

    ISBN 1-85091-655-1

Printed and bound in Great Britain by
Biddles Ltd, Guildford

Acknowledgements

I want to thank all those people who have, in a diversity of ways, helped somewhere in the creation of this book.

In particular I am conscious of: Valeria d'Alcantara, Susan Banham, Michael Brown, Philippa Colman, Cliff Comyns, Margaret Dunford, Dr George Hamber, Lynda Heath, Keith Herbert, Nicky Hill, Noel Hill, Ralph Homer, Patty Lake, Dr Paul Latawski, Karen Morrison, Joan Pilkington, Vaughan Schulze, and Geoff Smith.

The extracts from an essay on T S Eliot which appear on pp 42–4 and the examination questions on p 67 are reproduced by kind permission of the University of Cambridge Local Examinations Syndicate. The comments on relevance at the beginning of Chapter 6 owe their origin to feedback from the University of Oxford Delegacy of Local Examinations, whose careful, caring and helpful approach I have valued over many years. I am grateful to Stephen Wall, Fellow of Keble College, Oxford, for being happy to allow me to reproduce, on p 24, sentences from his essay on *Coriolanus*.

A Level success can best come from an environment which helps students to develop their potential in a balanced, caring and happy community. I am indebted to the Governors, the Headmaster and all who work and study at Moira House, for creating just such an atmosphere, from which this could spring.

I thank the following consultants for the valuable suggestions made from their rich understanding: Dr Philip Hills, formerly Director of the Primary Communications Research Centre in the University of Leicester, and until recently Senior Research Associate in the University of Cambridge; Dr Andrew Melhuish, a specialist in work and health, Medical Officer to the Administrative Staff College, Henley; Christine Raafat, Principal Psychologist, Eastbourne Health Authority; and Ralph Tabberer, an authority on information skills.

I am indeed thankful to June Lines, Senior Editor, Kogan Page Ltd, for her high level of sensitive and insightful guidance.

ACKNOWLEDGEMENTS

I do wish to express my warm thanks to Dr Philip Hills for his wider role of support and encouragement. Notwithstanding his many commitments, he has given generously of his time in long discussions, and without his presence I would not have ever embarked on study skills writing.

The responsibility for what is written is of course mine.

Howard Barlow
May 1985

Contents

Acknowledgements   **5**

Preface to the Second Edition   **9**

How to Use this Book   **11**

1. Starting A Levels   **13**
    1.1   Enjoying your subjects **13**
    1.2   Group discussion **14**
    1.3   Group phenomena **15**
    1.4   Working on your own **16**
    1.5   Thinking **17**

2. Reading   **21**
    2.1   Search skills **21**
    2.2   Types of reading **22**
    2.3   Quicker reading and better understanding **23**

3. Notes and Essays   **26**
    3.1   Making notes **26**
    3.2   Alternatives to notes **31**
    3.3   Personal choice in notes **37**
    3.4   Writing essays **39**
    3.5   Personal choice in essays **41**

4. Revision Notes   **45**
    4.1   Making revision notes **45**
    4.2   Variations on revision notes **47**
    4.3   Personal choice in revision notes **48**

5. Time   **52**
    5.1   Time and revision **52**

        First year
    5.2   The first term of A Levels **52**
    5.3   Getting work done during term time **53**
    5.4   Consolidating work during term time **55**
    5.5   The Christmas holiday **55**
    5.6   Spring term **55**
    5.7   Spring holiday **55**
    5.8   Dealing with mid-course lack of motivation **56**
    5.9   Summer term **56**
    5.10 Summer holiday **57**

Second year
5.11   Autumn term **57**
5.12   The Christmas holiday **57**
5.13   Spring term **60**
5.14   Spring holiday **60**
5.15   Summer term **60**

General points
5.16   Sleep **61**
5.17   Recreation **62**
5.18   Managing stress **62**
5.19   Handwriting **62**
5.20   Grammar and spelling **65**

6. The Examination   **67**
6.1   Relevance **67**
6.2   Tackling the paper **69**
6.3   Writing essays in the exam room **69**
6.4   Answering multiple-choice questions **72**
6.5   The examiner's task **73**

7. The Psychology of Study   **74**
7.1   Motivation **74**
7.2   Thinking **75**
7.3   Memory **76**
7.4   Approaches to learning **77**
7.5   Ways of learning **78**
7.6   The SQ3R method **80**

8. Coursework   **81**
8.1   Three golden rules **81**
8.2   Choosing a topic **81**
8.3   Doing the research **82**
8.4   Writing up your study **87**
8.5   Experiments **90**

9. Courses and Careers   **92**
9.1   Picking the right A Levels, AS Levels and extra GCSEs **92**
9.2   What to do after A Levels **98**
9.3   Getting into Oxford or Cambridge **100**
9.4   Choosing university courses and other training **101**
9.5   Planning a fall-back **104**
9.6   Completing a good application form **105**
9.7   Doing well in an interview **106**
9.8   Waiting for the results **109**
9.9   When the results come out **109**

Index   **112**

Preface to the Second Edition

The whole text has been revised and expanded to keep abreast of current developments. In particular, there is extra emphasis on the skills of thinking and on learning in groups, the 'gap year' is covered, there is more on Oxbridge, and a new chapter on coursework. There is a new section on the issue of the results.

I have taken account of the new GCSE and AS Level examinations. Dr Clive Wake, Secretary to the Standing Conference on University Entrance, generously read section 9.1, pp 92–7, dealing with A Level and AS Level choice. I am most grateful for his assurance about the views expressed, though I take responsibility for what is said.

The University of London School Examinations Board kindly allowed me to reproduce, on p 32, an annotated diagram from their publication *Subject Reports*, June 1984.

I am grateful to Donald Markwell, Fellow of Merton College, Oxford, for inviting me to talk with students at Merton on my research into undergraduate study habits and attitudes. I was at the time revising this book, and drew much stimulus from my visit.

Howard Barlow
May 1988

How to Use this Book

Before your A Levels start
9.1   Picking the right A Levels, AS Levels and extra GCSEs **92**
8   Coursework chapter **81–90**

1st year sixth: autumn
1.1   Enjoying your subjects **13**
1.2   Group discussion **14**
1.3   Group phenomena **15**
1.4   Working on your own **16**
7.4   Approaches to learning **77**
5.1   Time and revision **52**
5.2   The first term of A Levels **52**
5.3   Getting work done during term time **53**
5.4   Consolidating work during term time **55**
2.1   Search skills **21**
2.2   Types of reading **22**
3.1   Making notes **26**
3.2   Alternatives to notes **31**
3.3   Personal choice in notes **37**
3.4   Writing essays **39**
3.5   Personal choice in essays **41**
5.5   The Christmas holiday **55**

1st year sixth: spring
5.6   Spring term **55**
1.5   Thinking **17**
9.2   What to do after A Levels **98**
9.3   Getting into Oxford or Cambridge **100**
2.2   Types of reading **22**
2.3   Quicker reading and better understanding **23**
5.19   Handwriting **62**
5.20   Grammar and spelling **65**
5.7   Spring holiday **55**
4.1   Making revision notes **45**
4.2   Variations on revision notes **47**
4.3   Personal choice in revision notes **48**

1st year sixth: summer
5.9   Summer term **56**
5.8   Dealing with mid-course lack of motivation **56**
9.4   Choosing university courses and other training **101**
9.5   Planning a fall-back **104**
5.10   Summer holiday **57**
2.2   Types of reading **22**
2.3   Quicker reading and better understanding **23**
7.6   The SQ3R method **80**

HOW TO SUCCEED IN A LEVELS

2nd year sixth: autumn

5.11	Autumn term	**57**
9.6	Completing a good application form	**105**
7.1	Motivation	**74**
7.2	Thinking	**75**
7.3	Memory	**76**
7.5	Ways of learning	**78**
9.7	Doing well in an interview	**106**
5.1	Time and revision	**52**
4.1	Making revision notes	**45**
4.2	Variations on revision notes	**47**
4.3	Personal choice in revision notes	**48**
5.12	The Christmas holiday	**57**

year sixth: spring

5.13	Spring term	**60**
5.14	Spring holiday	**60**

2nd year sixth: summer

5.15	Summer term	**60**
5.16	Sleep	**61**
5.17	Recreation	**62**
5.18	Managing stress	**62**
5.19	Handwriting	**62**
6.1	Relevance	**67**
6.2	Tackling the paper	**69**
6.3	Writing essays in the exam room	**69**
6.4	Answering multiple-choice questions	**72**
6.5	The examiner's task	**73**
9.8	Waiting for the results	**109**
9.9	When the results come out	**109**

Chapter 1
Starting A Levels

This book is designed mainly to help A Level (and Scottish Higher Grade) students, though its content is applicable to any advanced student or mature student both in the United Kingdom and overseas.

Although what is said stems from close contact with advanced students over some 20 years, I have nevertheless been careful to ensure that this book does not merely reflect my own experiences but is also founded on a firm research and psychological base. Even so, it is a *view*, not a *prescription*. Its aim is to help you develop your own successful approach to your work.

1.1 Enjoying your subjects

A Levels and AS Levels are exciting! For a start, you can choose the ones you like best, and pp 92–7 will help you make your choice. But enjoyment in depth comes from really cherishing your subjects, or really 'getting into them'. This involves *personal* commitment and going *beyond* the standard sessions. For example:

1. *English Literature*. Success requires your own *personal* engagement with, and response to, the texts. Hence knowledge of the texts is paramount. *Beyond* the set texts, there are other books by the authors to be read, and books by other writers in those genres, as well as theatre visits.
2. *Modern Languages*. A visit to the country where the language is spoken is an enormous help. This can be arranged through an exchange scheme with a school or a family. Such visits not only increase one's standard of oral capability, they also develop an active and intelligent interest in the country's life and institutions, thus generating the use of more abstract and evaluative language (the distinguishing mark of an A Level candidate). Seeing foreign films and listening to relevant broadcasts widen one's knowledge of the country and language.
3. *Geography*. Fieldwork is an essential element. Journals are an essential supplement to formal reading in order to keep up to

date, for Geography is a developing subject. For example, to study Western Europe it is necessary to be aware of EEC policies and their implementation.

4. *Art*. A good knowledge of the history of art is most helpful, whether or not there is a specific paper on it in your A Level. Visits to museums and exhibitions widen and deepen awareness even if no notes are taken.

5. *Sciences*. Practical work becomes more important, and gives scope for personal observation and individual initiative. A Biology dissection involves drawing what you actually see (aided by a hand-held lens), rather than drawing what you think you should see. In a Physics practical, a preliminary investigation of the range of values possible is helpful in determining the intervals at which readings are to be taken. After the graph has been plotted, a further check of readings or additional values may well be essential to determine more precisely the shape of the line. Chemistry experiments involve careful and precise observation on your part. You infer a conclusion from your observations and test your inference by performing an experiment of your own devising. The onus is on you. Do read scientific journals. Arguably, the processes of modern science can barely be understood without a sense of the tradition of experiment and making research public.

1.2 Group discussion

Group discussion is important because it generates understanding of material. It also stimulates. But being a member of a group is not necessarily easy.

As a group member, you face a conflict. On the one hand, you can withdraw from the group into silence; you are then safe but you feel isolated. On the other hand, you can become involved in the group by speaking; this is fine when people agree with you and you feel elated, but when they disagree, feel hostile or think you foolish, you can feel somewhat persecuted and rejected.

The solution is to develop a realistic but positive *attitude* towards groups. This involves the following:

1. Prepare in advance. This remedies lack of knowledge.
2. Be friendly.
3. Expect both agreement and disagreement, but see them both as leading to creativity and progress.
4. Organise and write up jottings taken during the discussion.

Next, be sure to help the group to *develop*. This is a sensitive and important task. You should:

1. Be receptive. Listen attentively. Interest shown, even if silently, is a positive contribution. Make sure you can see everyone, as you need to take in not just what people say, but also their facial expressions and gestures. Circular or rectangular seating arrangements are best.
2. Ask people to clarify what they mean if you are unclear.
3. Raise a question to which you do not know the answer. Lack of knowledge is an opportunity to learn, not a problem to be hidden.
4. Summarise what has been said when you feel the discussion needs pulling together.
5. Help with group silence. Silence can be productive, when material is being digested. But if it is unproductive, and extends beyond its natural limit, try to put into words what you think the problem is. Perhaps the topic is too hard, or unmentionable, or there is temporary friction between group members. Verbalisation of the problem promotes its resolution.

Finally, make a *contribution*:

1. Isolate a key idea mentioned and elaborate on it.
2. Suggest a new line.
3. Give your opinions, and the evidence that goes with them, though without taking all the limelight. Your opinions are what you'll need in the exam room and in life: by giving them to the group, you will find they come back improved and developed.
4. When giving a talk, use brief notes only, then your own words. Do not write it out in full. The delivery of a good talk should be in the same natural style as you use for answering the questions at the end.

1.3 Group phenomena

There are some group phenomena which you will come to recognise. They are:

1. *Dependency*. This is where everyone expects the teacher to provide all the answers. Students seem to feel they know nothing and have nothing to contribute.
2. *Pairing*. Two members of the group can pair up in dialogue. Everyone else listens on the sidelines.

3. *'Fighting'*. A kind of 'fighting' can occur in groups as when an attack is made on, say, the syllabus or an alleged inadequacy in the public library.
4. *'Flight'* from the subject matter can occur, for instance by absence, lateness, senseless objections, idle chat or 'switching off'.

In an extreme form, these phenomena hinder the work of the group, and it is rare for them to be entirely absent.

The cure is to stick to the task of the group, then these phenomena will be harnessed to it. In general terms, the task is to find greater understanding of a topic through co-operative effort. The teacher, though in control, will tend to allocate him- or herself equal status with the students in order to aid this co-operation. More specifically, each session will have its own special task. It is important not to divert from the task on the vast majority of occasions, and allow only for the sporadic digression which, though irrelevant at the time, is truly productive in a wider sense.

1.4 Working on your own

The GCSE examination is designed for all students. A Levels and AS Levels are for those students who choose to stay in education beyond the school leaving age, to be followed in a good many cases by university or polytechnic. Hence A Levels feel different from GCSEs. The diagram opposite explains why.

A Levels are dependent to a much greater extent on students studying and learning independently. Work assignments are much more open ended. A subject called French, say, in the fifth form is not the same as a subject called French in the sixth. The teacher's expectations will be different. You have to pick up the new cues.

As A Levels require a personal understanding and appreciation in depth, it is understandable that private study is very important. You are your own taskmaster, under your own control, making your own decisions. It is my conviction that to be a winner, you have to work steadily throughout your course, but it is for you to judge that. You choose how and when you will study. You set your own balance between work and leisure. It is my hope that this book will help you move through this new phase. *How to Use this Book* on p 9 indicates which pages may be relevant at the various stages of your A Level career.

Why A Levels feel different from GCSEs

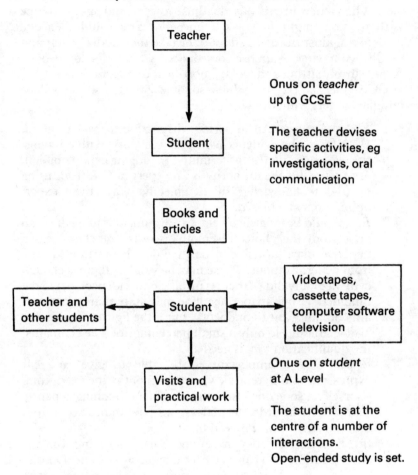

1.5 Thinking

A key aim at A Level is to develop as a pleasant person who thinks. The prime requirement is *intellectual curiosity*. This leads to intellectual conviction, which you then justify from evidence.

Being well read is a powerful stimulus to intellectual curiosity. Read widely, not only within your subjects but also outside them. Acquire a knowledge of current affairs: the 'leaders' in *The Times*, *Telegraph*, *Independent* and *Guardian* are useful. Try to include in your thinking morality, law, art, music and literature. Keep a cuttings book and an index: syllabuses are becoming increasingly topical.

Share your thoughts, advance a definite line and think on your feet. When a new idea is raised, adjust your mental jigsaw to cope with it. You might first ask a question. You could then cite evidence against the idea, adopt it, or take the middle course and modify your view. Suppose someone says Eliot is a lousy poet. Avoid simply sitting and looking horrified; think and respond.

GCSE has helped you to think, so some of the techniques will be familiar; others will be new.

1. *Fact and opinion.* An important distinction to bear in mind. With facts, the evidence *amounts to* certainty; with opinions, the evidence *falls short of* certainty. In judging expert opinion, ask yourself if the authority is an expert in that field, using up-to-date knowledge in an objective way. Even expert opinion may be biased.

2. *Bias* should be identified before an argument is judged. It can arise from the choice of emotive words: 'rebellion' has a negative bias, 'uprising' a positive one. Bias can also arise from generalisations. These may be valid (if there is enough evidence), invalid (if there is insufficient evidence), or valid if qualified. A newspaper headline may state that dole claimants do not want to find work, but if the figures cited in the article amount to only a small percentage of dole claimants, the qualification *some* is needed.

3. *Empathy.* It is important to be able to give coherent expression to different viewpoints. Empathy means putting yourself in someone else's shoes (while remaining separate from them) in order to understand how things seem from their point of view. Proceed thus:

   (a) Express how they *feel.* A vocabulary of feeling words is essential. You can make a table, using the one opposite as a start. Use your own opinion. Be alert to the precise shade of meaning each word has. This is usually clear from the word's root, so use a detailed dictionary.

   (b) Understand their *situation.*

   (c) Link their *feeling* with their *situation.* For example, a woman in a factory may feel oppressed. Her situation is a machine environment. Thus one could say: 'She feels oppressed because she is working in a machine environment.'

Empathy means understanding, not judging, which is a separate process where you bestow values. Nor is it the same as sympathy, which implies feeling pity and wanting to help. Sympathy and empathy may or may not go together.

Table of some feeling words useful for empathy work

	Words describing feeling good	Words describing feeling bad
Strong	exultant elated jubilant joyous	distraught aggrieved depressed oppressed
Medium	happy glad cheerful optimistic	despondent deflated downhearted apprehensive
Weak	pleased fortunate contented satisfied	troubled miserable bemused uneasy

4. *Conceptual thinking*
   'Is Britain a member of the EEC?'
        is a question of *fact*.
   'Should Britain belong to the EEC?'
        is a question of *judgement*.
   'Do you feel yourself to be a European?'
        is a question of *concept*.

   You must first set out the criteria which make up a European-feeling person. Go for the crucial criteria, the points that really matter. In deciding on the criteria, think of clear-cut cases falling both within, and outside, the concept; don't forget to include the negative angle, a most useful angle in all thinking. You may sometimes need to provide two analyses of a concept, one which includes the case in question, and one which does not. Questions can be both of judgement and of concept (eg, 'Should you feel yourself to be a European?'). The classic work on conceptual thinking is: Wilson, J (1963) *Thinking with Concepts*, Cambridge: CUP.
   Individual A Levels have their own special concepts for detailed analysis, eg the concept of irony in English Literature.
5. *Moral thinking.* Issues of right and wrong often arise in discussion. It is useful to bear in mind some moral systems. The Rights Theorist might cite the United Nations Declaration of Human Rights, while the Biblical Fundamentalist

19

will refer to the literal words of the Bible. The Cultural Relativist holds that there are no right or wrong answers to moral problems: cultures develop their own standards and cannot be compared. The Utilitarian believes an action is right which produces the greatest good for the greatest number, while an Agent-Centred Theorist might look at the motivation of the doer, and argue that an action is right if it is right-motivated. A Situationist may argue that each situation must be treated separately, and that the right action must be felt out. It is an interesting exercise to think through the implications of each standpoint.

6. *Problem solving.* This is very much a part of the GCSE examination. You will have done a good deal of it; for example investigations in Mathematics. The steps behind all problem solving are worth bearing in mind:

    (a) Objective. What am I trying to achieve?
    (b) Givens. What am I told?
    (c) Operations. How can I manipulate what I'm told?
    (d) Conclusion. What is my result?

    Problems are best solved step by step.

7. *Decision making.* This is a specialised form of problem solving which you will use, for example, when you decide what to do after A Levels. Again, a step-by-step policy is effective:

    (a) Problem. What exactly is the problem?
    (b) Alternatives. What is my evaluation of the alternatives?
    (c) Priority. What are the priorities which the decision must meet?
    (d) Choice. Which alternative do I choose?
    (e) Action. What action must I now take?

Chapter 2

Reading

You will find one theme running through this chapter: the importance of structure. All knowledge is stored and presented in a structured way, and the effective acquiring of knowledge depends on recognising that structure.

Structure is important in other fields too. Andrew Lloyd Webber, the composer of the music for *Jesus Christ Superstar* and *The Phantom of the Opera*, made the point that '. . . structure is the most important thing in a musical. Of course the content has to be good too, but you can have the most marvellous song in the wrong place in a show, and it can be a complete disaster. Equally, you can have some indifferent material that comes across very well because the show is so cleverly constructed.'

2.1 Search skills

A library can be a daunting place. You can feel quite at sea there. But there are some typical landmarks in a library. They will be marked on a floor plan, which you should study. A common layout is:

The microfiche viewer (which has taken over from the card catalogue in many libraries) looks rather like a television screen. It contains film negatives with information classified by author, by title and by subject. They enable you to trace the book's number (Dewey Decimal System), after which you can find the book on the shelf.

Everyone has some familiarity with libraries, but too many people drift around them without realising their structure and the structure of the information they contain.

Once you have found the book, you need to judge its worth. Is it up to date? Who is the author? Is there bias? What does the table of contents look like? What does the preface say?

2.2 Types of reading

Once you have found your material, you have to choose the right style for reading it. There are more styles of reading than just 'ordinary reading'. Your choice of reading style will depend on what you require from the material:

1. *Browsing* means looking through a book in a leisurely way. It is useful when you are just beginning to get to grips with a new area, because it helps you to acquire a general idea and to formulate better search questions. It is also useful for wide reading. To browse, you open the book, explore and read parts here and there.

2. *Rejection.* Have the confidence to reject a book you do not like, then find another. Students' reluctance to reject a resource is often at the root of their inefficiency or ineffectiveness. There may be a few books from which you cannot escape, but you have much more latitude and choice than is usually realised. Do not assume that a well known book is a 'must' for you even if you don't like it. It is a very high priority to find books which you like.

3. *Scanning* means searching for a definite piece of information. Look up the item in the index and write down *all* the page numbers on a slip of paper (this is much quicker than looking up the item several times in the index). Then scan over the relevant pages to find the information you want.

4. *Skimming* means glancing over a chapter quickly, extracting only the main points. Skimming is selective reading: you look over the chapter and select certain bits to read. In particular, you read the first sentences of each paragraph. They contain much information, and tell you which lines to focus your

attention on to obtain the information you want. You also look at: the introduction of the chapter, its headings, tables, pictures, diagrams and conclusion. But you will tend to do this automatically if you read the first sentences of each paragraph. Skimming is a useful, respectable but much-neglected practice.

When writing an essay, the use of a short, simple chapter to find your bearings, coupled with points skimmed from a good range of sources, can produce an effective result. Unquestionably the key skill to practise is skimming. It is important not only in its own right for 'gutting' a chapter, but also as the first step in intensive reading: quick skimming gives you a good general idea of the text as a skeleton on which to base a closer and complete reading. It is the hallmark of a good reader. To illuminate the value of skimming, the first sentences of paragraphs from an article on *Coriolanus* are shown on p 24. Read them carefully.

If you were using skimming to extract the main points on the political angle of the play, you would realise you need to read the second paragraph only; if you were using skimming as the first step in intensive reading to gain a complete mastery of the article, then you would have an excellent idea of the content before detailed reading.

2.3 Quicker reading and better understanding

There has been much study and research into the improvement of reading, but as yet not total agreement on how this can be done. However, one way of describing what happens when a good reader reads is in terms of the conducted coach tour. The coach drives smoothly past the sights of interest at quite a fast speed, though it slows down when there is much of importance to see. The traveller does not attend equally to everything he passes; he takes in especially the main sights, on which the guide gives a commentary.

There are a number of important points that arise from this metaphor:

1. Move your eyes *smoothly* across the lines. Actually, they move in little jumps, but don't think of it like that. Think of moving them smoothly across the lines. In this way you hold the drift of the argument in the forefront of your mind, and cut out looking back over the last few words (called regression).

Coriolanus was probably first performed in 1608. _____
_____
_____

Although *Coriolanus* is deeply concerned with politics, it remains uncertain what Shakespeare's own position was, if any._____
_____
_____

Coriolanus is certainly a play that provokes interference: the hero is markedly less sympathetic than Shakespeare's tragic heroes usually are, and it has often been felt that something must be done to make up for this supposed inadequacy._____
_____

It is true that the audience does not often feel close to Coriolanus; not many people on the stage do either._____
_____
_____

The person who finally stops Coriolanus in his revengeful tracks is the person who first set him on his destructive course, his mother.
_____
_____

The combination of forces which finally defeats Coriolanus is formidable. _____
_____
_____

Most of Shakespeare's tragic heroes have too much human feeling for their own good; Coriolanus seems to have too little._____
_____
_____

Skimming: from an article on Coriolanus, showing only the first sentences of paragraphs (not to scale).

Read groups of words: these contain the thought units. Let punctuation help you.

2. Move your eyes across the lines *as quickly as you can*, but their speed of movement must vary according to the nature of the text. A difficult text must be taken more slowly.

3. Hear your *inner voice speaking the key words*. Many words on a page are very common ones, such as 'the' and 'a'. We see them so often that we understand them by sight alone. It is the less familiar words which need to be heard. Hearing can be confined to a very limited proportion of words, but this is achieved by only the fastest readers.

   NB. With inner speech, your lips and vocal chords do not actually move: that would be subvocalisation. Subvocalisation tends to limit your reading rate to that of speaking, and should be avoided.

4. *Don't get too close to the book.* If reading is a type of sightseeing, you fail to appreciate the view if you are too close. Keep the book away from you so that you can take in the groups of words more easily. If you are not using a pile of books as a book rest, and are holding the book tilted backwards, the bend in your arm should be about 120 degrees. Distance also cuts out side-to-side head movements, which are tiring.

These points will need practising. Here is a formula which summarises what to do to improve your reading technique:

> **HOLD THE BOOK AT BENT ARM'S LENGTH.**
>
> **MOVE YOUR EYES SMOOTHLY ACROSS THE LINES AS FAST AS THE TEXT WILL ALLOW.**
>
> **HEAR YOUR INNER VOICE SPEAK THE KEY WORDS.**

Chapter 3

Notes and Essays

The next concern is the importance of structure in the setting out and recording of knowledge, that is to say, the importance of structure in notes and essays.

3.1 Making notes

Notes are made, rather than taken. Note making is a creative process. It involves *judging* the relevance of material to your objective, *rejecting* what is not relevant, *selecting* the important points and *fusing* the chosen material into a new structure.

It is unfortunate that the word 'note' carries the connotation 'scrappy'. A good note is exactly the opposite: it is organised, or structured, with great care, and the structure must be readily apparent. In this way the mind can grasp the note. Note making is the imposition of your own structure on to chosen material.

Before making a note, it is essential to have your objective very clear in your mind. Otherwise you do not know what to reject; everything seems important. There is a theory of management in industry called MBO (management by objective) which believes that you get things done by having clear objectives or targets.

One way of reading a chapter intensively and making notes on it is:

1. *Skim.* Acquire a general idea of the chapter by giving it a quick skim.
2. *Read.* Ideally, do not make notes at first, simply read for understanding. It is hard to make a good selection of material at this stage. Things noted now may seem unnecessary in retrospect. However, with a soft pencil, make light vertical marks in the margin opposite the points to which you will return. Now you don't feel you are missing anything. You do, of course, erase the marks at the end. Light pencil marks are suggested, and if made as described and later erased, less damage is done to books which are communal property than turning the pages.

3. *Scan.* Look back over the chapter to select information which is important to your objective. You now have the material in perspective and can select skilfully.

4. *Make notes.* This comes last. Note making is a recall activity. Tear up sheets of A4 paper into quarters. Write only on one side of each piece. Start a new piece of paper for each major point. When you have finished reading all the material, the pieces of paper can be grouped into small piles, each pile dealing with one aspect of the title. These piles become subheadings in the note.

   It is no use making notes from one book, then from another, and tacking the second set of points beneath the first on the same sheet of A4 paper. Material from different sources has to be integrated into one note. This takes time, but it is time well spent. While you are moving material around, you are thinking and learning. (For a fast lecture, write on one side of each sheet of paper and afterwards cut up the sheets into strips, then group them.)

Your notes should then be written out on loose-leaf file paper. Write on one side of each sheet only. Start a new sheet for a new topic. Restructuring of notes, and altering their order, is then possible.

The finished product could look like the example shown on p 30.

A television programme in two parts on the Common Market was seen. Notes were taken on one side of sheets of paper. The material from both programmes was cut up into pieces and similar material from both programmes was placed together in little piles. The piles were put in a logical order. They became the subheadings in the note, which is reproduced on pp 28–9.

An example of a note

THE COMMON MARKET

Background

1. Origin. WWI and WWII were European civil wars. They led to the notion of a 'United States of Europe' to prevent another European war. This notion was part of the thinking behind the EEC.

2. Treaty of Rome 1957
   (a) Initial members. France, Luxembourg, West Germany, Italy, Belgium, Netherlands.
   (b) Joined later. Britain, Ireland, Denmark (1973). Britain joined later because of her attachment to her Commonwealth. Greece (1981). Spain, Portugal (1986).

3. The working of the EEC
   (a) The Commission in Brussels. The original idea was that it should override government. This gave way to the idea that all government ministers must agree. Slow.
   (b) The European Parliament in Strasbourg. This is directly elected but has no power. It can only make representations.

Achievements

1. Economic. Movement between the countries of the EEC is much easier. Work permits are easily available to work in other EEC countries eg Italians work in Germany. There are no tariffs (import duties) within the EEC; this means bigger markets for EEC countries and W Germany particularly has been helped by this. Some goods are cheaper abroad eg cars. These can be as much as £1,500 cheaper abroad in the EEC. People go over for a day to get one.
2. Political. In the Falklands crisis, the US was not sure which side to support but the EEC backed Britain, and imposed economic sanctions on Argentina. Europe thus acted in unison. No more European arms were sent to Argentina. Some of the idealism about a united Europe has faded since 1957 because of bickering about economic issues, and it is unlikely that Europe will 'denationalise', but the countries of the EEC will become better at working together. Europe will emerge as a third world power to balance USA and USSR.

Problems

1. Food. Many French rural areas have poor farmers. They need financial help or people would leave and the countryside would be deserted; also, there are no jobs for farmers to go to if they did leave. So high prices for food are guaranteed by the EEC. This means overproduction, for a guaranteed high price spurs producers. A surplus results, which is sold off cheaply outside Europe. More of the EEC budget goes on agriculture than on anything else. Even the British farmer gets help — which he does not really need. Each European cow is subsidised by £100 a year.

2. Fishing. Continentals have fished out their own waters and Iceland has imposed a 200-mile limit: all these pressures send EEC fishermen into British waters. However, parts of Devon and Cornwall depend on fishing, and without it there will be 'ghost villages'. Our fishermen want a 12-mile limit. The limit is 6 miles.

3. Our contribution. £5,000m in 1987. For each £2 we pay in, we get only £1 back.

4. Protection. The use of national regulations to keep foreign goods out. This happens with food — we kept out foreign turkeys, Christmas 1982. Sometimes there are good reasons eg health, but some countries make up national regulations to keep out foreign goods eg British lawnmowers are noisy — the Germans use this to keep them out. The Commission is trying to harmonise rules and regulations.

5. Loss of identity. Eg we no longer have pounds, shillings and pence, just pounds and pence. We feel absorbed into 'Europe'.

6. Ignorance. People know very little about the EEC. This will improve.

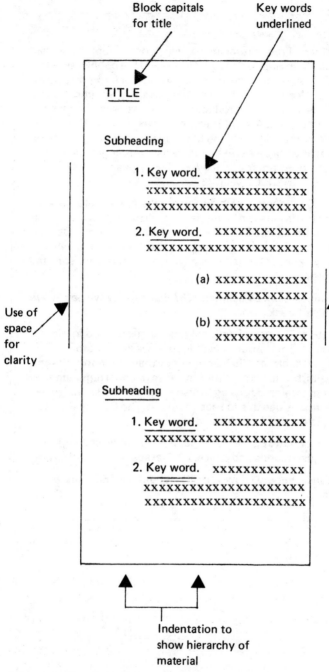

A blueprint for the structure of a note

For Maths notes, it is particularly important to include verbal explanation. This is often overlooked. The ideal structure of a Maths note is:

Instruction (to perform an operation)	Working out (with equals signs aligned)	Explanation (or comment)
Integrate between the limits O and Q	$W = \int_{0}^{Q} V dQ$	
	$W = \int_{0}^{Q} \dfrac{Q}{C} dQ$	where C is a constant
	$= \tfrac{1}{2} \, Q^2 / C$	

For vocabulary notes, it is better to go beyond just word and meaning, and adopt the following structure:

Word	Sentence	Meaning	Association (for memory)
emploi	Beaucoup de mes amis vont quitter l'école en juillet pour trouver un emploi.	job	employment

3.2 Alternatives to notes

There are alternatives to traditional notes. Your personal preference and the nature of your task may from time to time encourage you to use them.

1. *Annotated diagrams,* for example, the sketch map in Geography, and the drawing in Biology.
   (a) Make a clear diagram of the *structure*, keeping it simple, without excessive detail. This is vital.
   (b) Add annotations. An annotation is a written comment at the end of a specific labelling line. It talks about the *function* of the structure indicated.

Annotated diagrams relate structure to function. For example, an annotated sketch map could bring out the relationship between the physical geography of an area and its communications. They save long prose accounts, and have visual appeal. Rate them highly. Remember to include a title. In an exam, do not repeat in prose what your annotated diagram has already conveyed. The map opposite is the kind of thing to accompany a map work answer at A Level. Usually, an annotated diagram would be simpler, like the one of Ullapool below, which was quickly produced and which scored high marks in an examination.

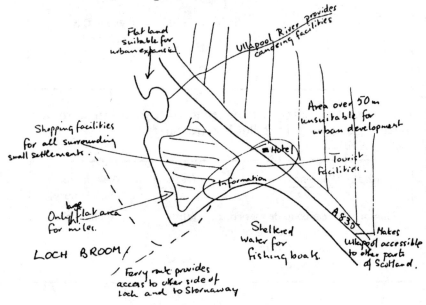

Annotated sketch map of Ullapool

2. *Patterns*. Tony Buzan has developed a method of note making called patterns. A pattern on the US political system, made up on Buzan lines, is shown on p 34. A pattern is a web spreading out from a topic written in the centre of the page. Related ideas are printed on lines drawn from the topic. If you make a pattern, it is useful to remember these pointers:

   (a) Keep it simple – try to write only two words per line.
   (b) Print – it's clearer.
   (c) Make your web lines from the box veer horizontally – it's easier to write on them.

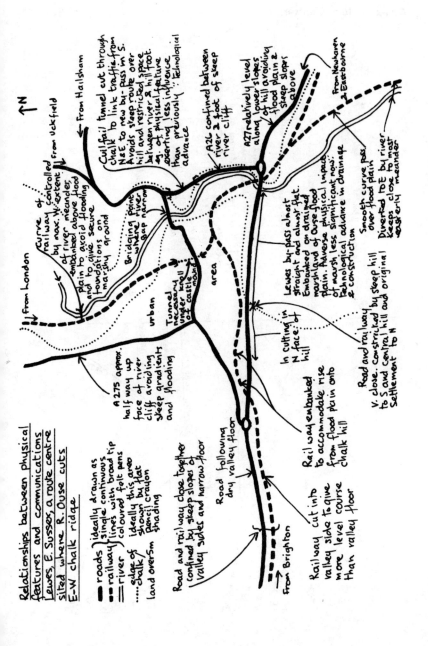

Relationships between physical features and communications Lewes, E. Sussex, a route centre sited where R. Ouse cuts E-W chalk ridge

— roads ⎱ ideally drawn as
━━ railway ⎰ single continuous lines with broad tip
══ river
···· edge of Chalk
land over 5m coloured felt pens ideally this area shown by flat coloured crayon shading

↑N

From London

curve of railway controlled by max W. extent at river meander embanked above flood plain to avoid flooding and to give secure foundations on marshy ground

From Hailsham

from Uckfield

Cuilfail tunnel cut through chalk to link traffic from N&E to new by-pass in S. Avoids steep route over hill and restricted space between river & hill foot e.g. a) physical feature asserting less influence than previously b) technological advance

A2c confined between river & foot of steep river cliff

A27 relatively level along lower slopes of hill avoiding flood plain & steep slopes above

From Newhaven & Eastbourne

Bridging point where river gap narrows

Tunnel beneath upper castle mound

urban area

A275 approx. half way up face of river cliff avoiding steep gradient and flooding

Road following dry valley floor

Road and railway close together confined by steep slopes of valley sides and narrow floor

Leaves by-pass almost straight and almost flat. Embanked on drained marsh/dry of Ouse flood plain. Adverse physical impact of marsh less significant now: technological advance in drainage & construction

Smooth curve pass over flood plain

Diverted NE by river keeps close to most easterly meander

In cutting in N. face of hill

Road and railway v. close. Constricted by steep hill to S and central hill and original settlement to N

Rail way embanked to accommodate rise from flood plain onto chalk hill

From Brighton

Railway cut into valley side to give more level course than valley floor

An example of a pattern note

① Electoral College. Founding Fathers feared mob rule.

② Vice President and President.

③ First Tuesday in November.

④ Flexibility of commitment to specifics of platforms compared with rigid and ideological gulf between British party manifestos. Consensus is the key to understanding U.S. politics.

⑤ Elephant v. Donkey.

⑥ Youth, vigour, healthy life.

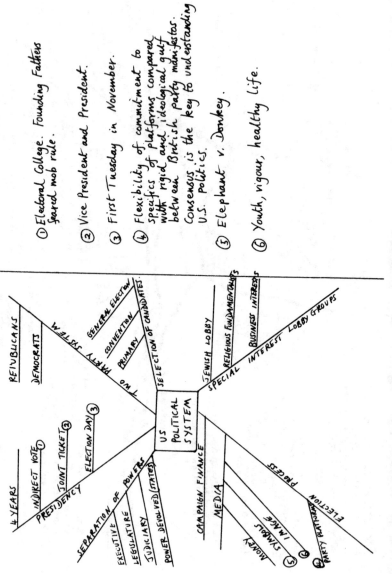

You read a chapter, making light pencil marks against the key points, then you make your pattern and rub out the pencil marks.

In my experience, students' reactions to patterns vary. I have not found them as popular as the standard method for coping with notes. Many students do not like them at all. On the other hand, I have known patterns used in English Literature to good effect. I use them to sort out ideas which seem muddled or confused, sometimes making an ordinary, linear note afterwards. I also use patterns for shopping, where each 'arm' is a shop to be visited, and the 'branches' are things to be bought there. Material from more than one source can be combined on to one pattern, which is a strength; essays can be planned using them, each 'arm' of the web forming a paragraph, with the 'branches' being the content of the paragraph. Patterns structure material effectively.

Buzan's ideas can be followed up in the following books, which are interesting reading:

Buzan, T (1974) *Use Your Head*, London: BBC Publications.
Buzan, T (1977) *Make the Most of Your Mind*, London: Colt Books.

Buzan has made people more aware of the value of linking ideas by lines. Some looser examples are given below and overleaf.

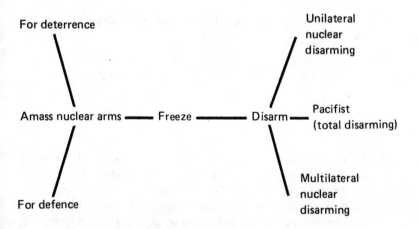

Pattern-type diagram showing positions on the nuclear issue

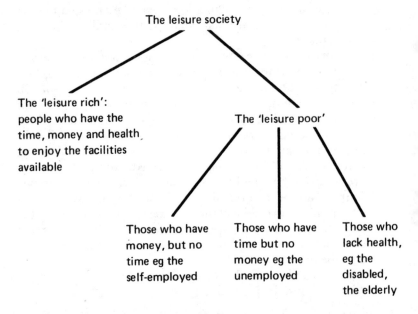

Pattern-type diagram showing society in the coming age of leisure

3. *Underlining.* If you *own* a book, and it needs to be mastered, underlining is a possibility. A method could be:

_____ Underline key phrases and key words.

✓ _____ Underline and tick parts to be learned by heart.

① ② ③ Put numbers in the text where a sequence of points occurs.

Underlining is not popular in Britain. It is rather lacking in creativity, and your ideas on what is important may change. However, I have known it used very effectively to master a set book.

4. *Flow charts.* A flow chart is a diagram consisting of a series of geometric shapes connected by arrowed lines. Each shape has a special use. The oval denotes 'start' or 'end'; the diamond asks a question; the rectangle does something. You will have met flow charts in your GCSE Mathematics, but they are useful in studying. They give a picture of how a procedure, system or sequence of events, operates. An example is shown on p 37. I have used a looser example on

Flow chart for Psychology A Level analysing why a child may not be at school

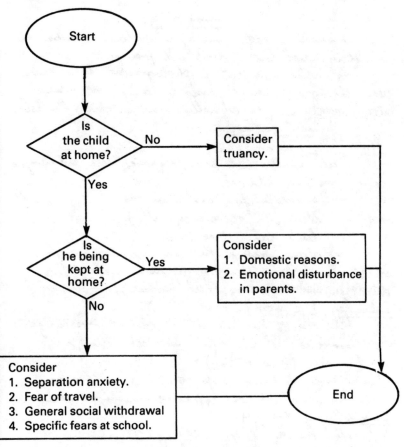

p 99. When making flow charts, start in the top left-hand corner of the page, as the direction of the flow lines is down the page and from left to right. Keep the questions in the diamonds as simple as possible, and remember that each should have only two possible answers, yes or no.

3.3 Personal choice in notes

An example is shown on p 38 of a note on Radioactivity made by a Physics A Level student who went on to read Dentistry at university. Numbering is not used, but there is a strong sense of layout, and the structure is readily apparent. The first side of the note is reproduced. I would prefer more use of space and a bigger diagram.

Radioactivity.

Emission of radiation by a radioactive subst. is completely independent of temp. and pressure.

This radiation affects a photographic plate, causes gases through which it passes to ionize, and makes certain substances (eg crystalline zinc sulphide) fluoresce.

Types of Radiation.

Alpha Rays (α rays)

These are attracted to a negative plate and therefore carry positive charges.

Have been identified as helium ions $^4_2He^{2+}$, in rapid motion (identified spectroscopically).

Very little penetrating power.

Very strong ionizing effect on any gas through which they pass. (This property most useful for detection and measuring their intensity).

Beta Rays (β- rays)

Attracted to positive pole ∴ carry a -ve charge. Beta particles (ie. e^- or $β^-$) are electrons in very rapid motion (mass = $\frac{1}{1836}$).

About 100 times as penetrating as alpha rays.

However, much less effective in ionizing gases.

Gamma Rays (γ-rays)

Unaffected by an electric field ∴ carries no charge. Gamma radiation is electromagnetic radiation of very high frequency. Resemble X rays but have an even shorter wavelength. Very great penetrative power.

A note on Radioactivity made by a Physics A Level student

3.4 Writing essays

Everyone has been taught at some time or other how to write an essay, and you may wonder what else there is to learn. Structure is the key principle, but used in a special way as follows.

The most important single point in essay writing is to answer the question in the first paragraph. Too often essays begin with a 'throat clearing' introduction which says nothing, or with an 'hors d'oeuvre' introduction, which is better but, as it merely gives some interesting background or quotations, does not go to the heart of the answer. You should give a clear answer to the question in the first paragraph, a 'nutshell' answer containing in miniature the key aspects which are to be developed in a structured way, paragraph by paragraph. If the essay ended after the first paragraph, it should be clear to the reader what your answer is.

The 'nutshell' answer in the first paragraph confers two large advantages. First, you know where you're going. You are forced to be relevant, and lack of relevance is a major reason for a poor essay. In this method, you know where you are going from the start; in other methods, you tend to feel your way towards an answer as you write, and you may divert from the question. Second, the reader knows where you're going. This is a considerable help to him, like a map on which he can see his journey before he begins it.

Having completed the answer in miniature in the first paragraph, you develop the touched-on aspects paragraph by paragraph. Each paragraph must deal with an aspect, and you must be able to say what that aspect is. In answering a question, you should assume knowledge on the examiner's part: you make allusion to material as far as the answer demands, but you do not need to fill out points beyond that.

In the conclusion, you restate the answer. This is not simply a 'replay' of the introduction; you restate the answer in the light of how you have developed your essay. It will thus be substantially the same but slightly different. It is essential to restate the answer to reinforce it in the reader's mind.

Here is an essay on the Common Market illustrating these points.

'We should leave the Common Market'. Discuss.

Answer in 'nutshell' form.

It would be a mistake to leave the Common Market. If we did so, it would be because of short-term problems such as agriculture and fishing. These can be solved in time, along with others such as our monetary contribution and EEC restrictive practices. In time these problems will recede, and we shall be more conscious of truly substantial long-term economic and political gains.

Agriculture and fishing problems.

Much of the negative publicity about the Common Market is about cows and fish. France, as an initial and powerful member of the EEC, established for herself and for European agriculture a system of subsidy under which, for example, each cow is financially supported to the sum of £100. Overproduction for guaranteed high prices causes 'butter mountains', which are sold at reduced rates outside the EEC, to the understandable anger of British people. But it is unlikely that a system so contrary to common sense will persist over time, although, inconsistently, we seek similar protection (though to a lesser extent) for our fishermen, who argue for a 12-mile limit to keep out Continental fishermen, who could soon turn parts of Devon and Cornwall into deserted villages. Fishing, as a more recent problem than agriculture, is likely to be more quickly solved, but the problem of agriculture will not deny resolution.

Money and restrictive practices problems.

Other problems, too, edge their way towards solution. We do not argue that we, as a country, should recoup in benefits the last penny of our annual financial contribution, but a return of £1 back for every £2 in is a situation with which our European partners sympathise. Nor are we happy when West Germany keeps out British lawnmowers on the pretence of their noise, though, again inconsistently, we are not beyond keeping out foreign turkeys at Christmas on 'health' grounds. However, the Commission is currently working to harmonise rules and regulations, and this problem is likely to be short-lived.

Economic gains.

More deep-rooted are the benefits and opportunities offered by the EEC membership in economic terms. Movement between the countries of the EEC is already much easier, and EEC work permits can be obtained. A number of British motorists have benefited by some

£1,500 in buying cars on the Continent, and from our industry's point of view, absence of tariffs makes Europe our market. The arrangement offers us an opportunity not a gift: our products must be substantial and at the right price. But this is an opportunity that British workmanship and the British worker are well able to take.

Political gains.

In world political terms, Britain has lost an Empire and not yet quite found a new soul. Though a late and somewhat reluctant member of the EEC, our future political identity lies within it. We may regret the passing of pounds, shillings and pence, but the EEC is for a 'United States of Europe' with nationalities intact, not for a 'Uniform Europe' with nationalities diminished. Already the ideal of a united Europe has found expression in reality: Europe supported Britain over the Falklands. We can have a new world role no less important than our last one, as part of a third world power block to lend stability to the balance of the superpowers.

Answer restated.

It would be a backward step without parallel to leave the Common Market. Budget bills, butter mountains and fishing limits seem large issues now, but they will have been forgotten among the economic and political benefits of the next century.

3.5 Personal choice in essays

Also reproduced are the first, second, fourth and sixth paragraphs of an essay on T S Eliot written by a grade A English Literature A Level student. It is common to indent quotations so they stand out from the main body of the essay; here there is very close reference to the text but it is interwoven into the main body of the essay. The structure of the essay is:

1st para	Answer in nutshell form.
2nd para	The poem 'The Love Song of J Alfred Prufrock'.
4th para	The poem 'The Waste Land'.
6th para	Answer restated.

'The occasional obscurity in Eliot's early poems is an important part of their effect.' What is your own view?

1st para

T.S. Eliot in his early poems makes far greater use of a technique which he later tended to abandon in favour of conveying the pure power of words themselves. This is the technique of using references to other poets or writers, even quoting directly from them, and references to myth or religion. Naturally, but for the initiated, those (and they must be few) with a scholarly knowledge equal to Eliot's own, his poems must seem obscure and sometimes incomprehensible. These references are, however, an important and intrinsic part of Eliot's poetry. Through them, he provides parallels or contrasts to the present, about which he is writing.

2nd para

'The Love Song of J. Alfred Prufrock' is built upon such references and images, although it has not the obscurity of parts of 'The Waste Land', which shows the culmination and climax of Eliot's use of this technique. Prufrock is a lonely man, isolated in a society which has debased its spiritual values, where people have become less than people, merely 'arms' or 'skirts that trail along the floor'. The epigraph is taken from Dante who influenced Eliot profoundly and the literary works upon which it is based are Marvell's 'To His Coy Mistress' and 'Hamlet'. Marvell's poem stresses continually the fleeting, transitory nature of time, and the need to squeeze all possible experience out of life. Prufrock, by direct contrast, has not 'the strength to force the moment to its crisis', his indecision is that of Hamlet, and his eternal cry is 'Indeed there will be time', even though he has seen 'the eternal footman hold my coat and snicker' and fears death. He can never attain the vitality and decision of

Marvell, and neither is he ' prince Hamlet nor was meant to be ', for he is no romantic hero, and Hamlet finally did 'force the moment to its crisis', and attained those heights of tragedy which are denied to Prufrock. These literary references are of vital importance to the effect of the poem. They compare a past age with the emptiness of the present, compare vitality and meaning (especially Marvell) with a depleted mankind.

4th para   'The Waste Land' is the climax of this technique. It is based on a framework of Shakespeare's 'The Tempest', and various references to ancient myths and fertility rites, particularly the legend of the Holy Grail, all of which hint at a possibility of rebirth and restoration. 'The Waste Land' is obscure, but the thoughts which Eliot is trying to convey are obscure and complex. Certainly the method can have its disadvantages. Sometimes Eliot's poetry is totally incomprehensible, and sometimes he seems to be enjoying academic 'in-jokes'. But in 'The Waste Land' the method gives unity to a long poem. Again the past contrasts with the sordid and depleted present. The 'sweet Thames' of Spenser's time is now reduced to a 'dull canal'. People, as in the preludes, are become bestial or inanimate, while objects and beasts take on human characteristics. The references give form to the poem, and hint continually at the possibility of redemption and restoration through faith, and willing surrender into it. The end of the poem is totally obscure, being a confusion of quotes and references, all of which still hint at the ultimate possibility of redemption although this has not yet been achieved. 'The Waste Land' without its network of reference and allusion would scarcely exist. It is given a rich and meaningful texture. The references provide contrasts with the present, and hint at the possibility of future redemption.

6th para   The obscurity of Eliot's poems can be considerable, but it is an important part of what he is trying to communicate. Reference and myth provide parallels and contrasts with the chaos and emptiness of modern living, and also give structure to the poems. The obscurity simply of language reflects the fact that it is often 'impossible to say just what I mean', that words are inadequate to express some of our deepest ideas and feelings.

Chapter 4

Revision Notes

It is now time to look at how the concept of structure can help with the consolidation of knowledge, and this brings us to consider revision notes, or summary notes, ie brief outlines of the material to be remembered.

4.1 Making revision notes

There are three key points to remember when making revision notes:

1. The *structure* of the revision note should be crystal clear. The outline should stand out clearly so that the development of the revision note strikes home as you look at it. The headings of the note should develop logically. A revision note can be compared with seeing a person through an X-ray. The skeleton is apparent and 'hangs together' as your eyes move downwards from head to toe.
2. *Large (A4) sheets of paper* are used. More can be contained on them and the structure of material more easily grasped. The paper can be unlined or have narrow lines. Going back to the skeleton image, one wants the whole skeleton on one piece of paper. Ideally, a whole topic (or a whole aspect of a topic) should have a side all to itself. Condensation of material on to a few sheets of paper is a large boost to confidence, for you no longer feel swamped by the quantity of material to be learned.
3. The revision note should contain some well chosen *landmark words*. These are key words which hint at the details to be remembered, and act as triggers or cues to areas of details within the overall structure. In the skeleton image, they would correspond to the key organs of the body.

Revision notes can be made throughout your course. You can make them for mid-course tests and these will probably be thrown away after they have served their purpose.

Nearer the end of your course, you will make your final revision notes. At this point your understanding of the material will have deepened, and you will be able to 'stand back' from it more easily. Revision notes made now will include only the very best material. They will be carefully organised. Having thought about them so much, you will virtually know the material on their completion, but you must then go for absolute mastery. You must *over*learn them.

A revision note can be mastered as follows. First look over the revision note as a whole, then break it down into as small 'wholes' or 'cells' as possible. Go over a 'cell', then try to recall it. You will have to recall it in the exam room, and it is as well to practise. When you cannot recall a point, it is safest to look straight away to avoid sowing guesses in your mind. Repeat and recall alternately. Master each small chunk before you go on to the next one but stick to short memory sessions, having many of them. When you have mastered each revision note in turn in this way, return to the first one and start all over again. Continue to learn them by this method even when you know them perfectly. Overlearning will help you to recall them under the pressure of the exam room.

There is no such thing as a model revision note. Any revision note is a model if it is felt to be of use by its maker. Some people prefer a spaced out, to a cluttered, format.

Here is a revision note on War Art. The main note appears first, followed by the revision note made from it.

WAR ART

Introduction

1. The film conveys continuing reality, and therefore has immediacy.
2. The photograph captures the split-second happening and emphasises seeing.
3. War art conveys feeling.

War art conveys feeling

1. Moore. He liked reclining figures. He portrayed people lying down in the tube during bombing. He conveys their feeling of weariness. The people and place fuse together to create the feeling of claustrophobia.
2. Searle. He drew the horrors of building a railway in the Far East. He conveys the feeling of barbarity.

War art uses symbolism

1. Nash. The devastated landscape in 'Menin Road' symbolises a

generation devastated by war. He combines realism and surrealism.

2. Spencer. He painted a picture of a pile of crosses, intermingled with soldiers and pack animals rising from the dead. Christ is the central figure in the heap. The crosses are a symbol. They are mass produced, thus a symbol of impersonality; and they are a symbol of hope of an after-life.

War art shows awareness of line

1. Nevinson's machine gunners painting uses straight lines and sharp angles to convey brutality. The gunners are dehumanised by the gun, hinting at the dehumanising effect of machine warfare. His control accentuates the terror.
2. Wyndham Lewis's 'A Battery Shelled'. The officers are detached and remote (curved lines); the men are tense under fire (angular lines).

War art can depict the less obvious sides of war

1. Ardizzone. He depicts humour: the Home Guard frisk an Englishman.
2. Sutherland. His 'Fallen Lift Shaft' notes beauty in destruction.

Revision note

WAR ART

Film cf photograph cf war art.

Feeling	—	Moore	(figures)	Searle	(railway)
Symbolism	—	Nash	(landscape)	Spencer	(crosses)
Line	—	Nevinson	(gunners)	Lewis	(battery)
Unobvious	—	Ardizzone	(frisking)	Sutherland	(beauty)

4.2 Variations on revision notes

There are three possible variations:

1. *Overmarking.* Some people like to mark over main headings and key points in their ordinary notes, using a special overmarking pen. This is useful if the structure is not clear.
2. *Margin notation.* Headings and key words can be written in the margin of ordinary notes. Again, this clarifies the structure if that is necessary.
3. *Index cards.* These can be used for revision notes instead of sheets of A4 paper. There is an example on p 48.

Their underlying principles are the same as for a standard revision note and if they work for you, use them.

An index card revision note

EDWARD VI 1547-1553

1) Elton: 'a cold-hearted prig' or his reign as full of 'disastrous policies or irresolute politicians'; the reduction of 'the king-worship of the early 16th to absurdity'.

2) Mackye - or Morris: could have turned out to be the most dazzling Tudor king.

3) Morris: the reign 'tested the constitutional engine constructed by H. VIII or T. Cromwell, or proved that it could survive reckless driving or could even survive being put into reverse.

4) Morris: 'S. might have done much for Eng., whereas Dudley brought her very near to ruin'.

5) Paget: 'Commons is become a king; a king appointing conditions or laws to the governors'.

4.3 Personal choice in revision notes

An index card made as part of revision for History A Level is shown above. For me, the material is not well structured: points are noted from different writers, but similar points should have been grouped together under headings. And inevitably with index cards, large areas of material cannot be taken in at a glance. Nevertheless the student found it helpful, which is what counts.

Page 49 shows one side of a nine-sided note for Pure Maths A Level, written by a student who went on to read Business Studies at university. It is clear and concise. An interesting point is the use of the split page, working down one column at a time. This is very suitable for Maths.

Pages 50 and 51 show the second half of a revision note on Dylan Thomas written by an A Level English Literature student who went on to read English at university. It deals with 'poetry and words', 'convention' and 'method' (the first half, which is of similar length, deals with 'birth', 'fruitfulness' and 'death'). The headings and subheadings are clear, and the student found it very helpful. It represents good condensation. My own inclination would be to try to condense more still, and to structure the material within subheadings in a more visually appealing way. I do not feel this strongly, though, and I would rate this a very solid revision note. The main point is that it helped the student.

Partial Fractions

1. $\dfrac{x}{(x+1)(x+3)}$ can be split

$\dfrac{x^2}{(x+1)(x+3)}$ divide 1st

2. $\dfrac{x}{(x+1)(x+3)} \equiv \dfrac{A}{x+1} + \dfrac{B}{x+3}$

3. $\dfrac{2x^2-3}{(x-1)^3(x+1)} \equiv \dfrac{A}{x-1} + \dfrac{B}{(x-1)^2} + \dfrac{C}{(x-1)^3} + \dfrac{D}{x+1}$

   N.B. Common denominator

4. $\dfrac{x+1}{(x-1)(x^2+1)} \equiv \dfrac{A}{x-1} + \dfrac{Bx+C}{x^2+1}$

Use of P.F.

1. Eg. expanding functions in ascending powers of x.

Work out P.F. to e.g. $\dfrac{1}{1-x} + \dfrac{x-1}{1+x^2}$

Binomial T. using $(1-x)^{-1} + (x-1)(1+x^2)^{-1}$

2. Integration.

Summation of Series

1. A.P. e.g. $1+2+3+4+\cdots+n$

$a=1 \quad d=1 \quad n=n$

$S_n = \dfrac{n}{2}(2 + (n-1)d)$

$\sum_{r=1}^{n} r = \dfrac{n}{2}(n+1)$

$\sum_{r=1}^{n} r^2 = \dfrac{n}{6}(n+1)(2n+1)$

$\sum_{r=1}^{n} r^3 = \dfrac{n^2}{4}(n+1)^2$

Integration by Substitution

1. $\int (1+2x)^{10} dx \qquad u = 1+2x$

2. $\int \sqrt{4-x^2}\, dx \qquad x = a\sin\theta$ i.e. $2\sin\theta$
   (a^2)

   $\dfrac{dx}{d\theta} = 2\cos\theta$

   $dx = 2\cos\theta\, d\theta$

   $\int \sqrt{4-4\sin^2\theta}\, d\theta$

   $\int 2\sqrt{1-\sin^2\theta}\,\, 2\cos\theta\, d\theta$

   $\int 2\cos\theta \times 2\cos\theta\, d\theta$

   $\int 4\cos^2\theta\, d\theta$

3. Odd powers of $\sin x \cdot \cos x$

   $u = \cos x$ for o.p. of $\sin x$

   $u = \sin x$ for o.p. of $\cos x$

   $\therefore \int \sin^5 x\, dx \qquad u = \cos x$

   $\int \sin^5 x \times \dfrac{du}{-\sin x} \qquad \dfrac{du}{dx} = -\sin x$

   $\int -\sin^4 x\, du$

   $\int -\sin^2 x\, \sin^2 x\, du$

   $-\int (1-\cos^2 x)(1-\cos^2 x)\, du$

   $-\int (1-u^2)(1-u^2)\, du$

4. e.g. $\int \dfrac{dx}{a+b\cos x}$ or $\int \dfrac{dx}{a+b\sin x}$

   $\cos x = \dfrac{1-t^2}{1+t^2}$

   $t = \tan\dfrac{x}{2}$

   $\dfrac{dt}{dx} = \dfrac{1}{2}\sec^2\dfrac{x}{2}$

   $= \dfrac{1}{2}\left[1 + \tan^2\dfrac{x}{2}\right]$

   $= \dfrac{1}{2}[1+t^2]$

   $dx = \dfrac{2\,dt}{1+t^2}$

   $\therefore \int \dfrac{dx}{2+\cos x} = \int \dfrac{2\,dt}{1+t^2} \times \dfrac{1}{\left[2 + \dfrac{1-t^2}{1+t^2}\right]}$

   $\int \dfrac{2\,dt}{3+t^2}$ standard form

Integration by Parts

$uv - \int v.\dfrac{du}{dx}.dx$

1. $\int \log x.dx \qquad u = \log x \quad \dfrac{dv}{dx} = 1$

   $\dfrac{du}{dx} = \dfrac{1}{x} \qquad v = x$

   $x\log x - \int 1\, dx \qquad \log x$ must $= u$ because

   $= x\log x - x + c \qquad$ it can't be integrated as v

2. Type of product involving using parts twice

   eg $\int x^2.\sin x\, dx$

   eg $\int e^x \sin x\, dx = -e^x\cos x + \int e^x\cos x\, dx$

   $= -e^x\cos x + e^x\sin x - \int e^x\sin x\, dx$

   $2\int e^x\sin x = -e^x\cos x + e^x\sin x$

   $\int e^x\sin x = \dfrac{-e^x\cos x}{2} + \dfrac{e^x\sin x}{2}$

Part of a revision note for Pure Maths A Level

HOW TO SUCCEED IN A LEVELS

POETRY & WORDS
① "Especially when the October wind"
  - Tyranny of words. "My busy heart who shudders as she talks
          sheds the syllabic blood and drains her words"
  - dependence on "heartless words"
  - should put more value on "neural meaning" deeper level.
  - listen to the message of the "dark vowelled birds"
  - to prevent words taking over + "the coming fury of Second
                                        coming"
                                      "centre cannot hold"
  - word has caused "crabbing sun" "a raven cough"
      "frosty fingers punish the land"
  - end of language
          "shut in a tower of words" (Ivory tower - detached)
② "The hand that signed the paper"
  - hands that write have "no emotion"
                "Hands have no tears to flow"
③ "Once it was the colour of saying"
        - desire for new poetry
        - yet "And every stone I wind off like a reel" (stone-hard,
                                              no feeling.)
④ "Hunchback in the Park"
        - desire for perfection "A woman figure without fault
                      Straight as a young elm"
⑤ "La Danseuse"
        - the dance so perfect "Her form was like a poet's mind"
⑥ "Light breaks where no sun shines"
        - new consciousness, deeper
        "Dawn breaks behind the eyes"
   Auden "All there is a voice"
⑦ "Time held me green & dying/Though I sang in my chains like the sea"   of words
                                                  "Fern Hill"
CONVENTION
① "I see the Boys of Summer"
  - Boys, destroy harvest, freeze seeds in soil, maid in love, destroy
    sweetness of summer with thoughts of Summer.
                              "I see the pulse of Summer in the ice"
                            "Of frozen loves they fetch their girls"
                          "There in the sun the frigid threads
                            of doubt and dark they feed their
                                              nerves"
  - with to oppose all, draw opposite out of everything
                "But seasons must be challenged"   opposition
  - convention of love + sex "A muscling-up from lovers in their cramp position"
                    "Here love's damp muscle dries - dies"
  - reversal . spring → Christmas "In spring cross our foreheads with holly"
        - earth "Hold up the noisy sea & drop their birds."

Part of a revision note on Dylan Thomas (and opposite)

③ "After the Funeral"
- convention of rel. "lie with religion in their cramp" c/f "I see"
- remove routine from life "... until

     The stuffed lung of the fox twitch and den here (now seen)
     And the stuffed fern lays seeds on the (barren)
            <u>black sill</u>"

- convention must bow down

     "Bow down the walls of the fenced dry woods"

<u>Fern Hill</u> "Now as I was young & easy under the apple boughs
    About the curly house & happy as the grass was green"
sound creates
    sense

<u>METHOD</u> ① Struggle of "stripping away darkness of struggling up to light"
    ② Feeling rather than thought. Not an intellectual poet, emotional.
    ③ Darkness to light Adam = sin → "upright Adam"
              Eden = garden where apple was eaten →
                      positive increase of the earth
              Flood = terror → refuge in the Ark

① First Period. personal problem – language limited / vocab small / repetitious /
                     obsession with few words "fork", "vein" "suck"
                  "worm" "deaths & other"
           – sentence short / short breathed / irregular
            in beat & length
            eg "If my head"

② "Second Period" charged with powerful & poignant feelings for others – luckier
           in vocab, words disfigure → red, longer grammatical
           units, eg 1 sentence of 8 stanzas in "Refusal ...."
           Symbols diminish → metaphors & images
③ Third Period – Faith and love – verbose, very long sentence / Adj on Adj /
           eloquence strong, one thought or emotion
           for whole poem, very bardic.

Ⓐ <u>Dialogue</u> "If my head ...." "removes hypothetical quality / more vivid
    (pseudo drama – several distinct people)

Ⓑ <u>Circumstantial ambiguity</u> – leaves us wondering, who, what, where
             when etc
            – not helped by title, only 2nd lines prompt even

Ⓒ <u>Orderly & Organised</u> – makes look closely
              – entertains emotion by regulating amount of knowledge
              – suspense
              – strong – plenty of meaning "sum . city 'sodom'city
                    full of sin → sodomy
              – old names "bow and arrow birds" – weather cock

- welshness
- bardic quality welsh love of music
- surrealism – wayardness (not a surrealist then a surrealist)
      – not a 'angry young man' 'But today the struggle'
GENERAL "private social poet" The conscious acceptance of guilt is necessary

like Christ all die achieve immortality for "After the first .... " AUDEN

Chapter 5

Time

5.1 Time and revision

Throughout our discussion on time, one theme will keep emerging: the need for revision. Much of our learning is lost because of lack of revision, and the reason that we can recall languages more than other school knowledge is because, while learning them, words and constructions are being revised automatically all the time. There is a tragic pattern: students spend hours gathering material; near the exam they find that there is too much to learn so they cut out some; they then see questions on the exam paper which they could have answered if they had learned all their notes. Revision throughout the course will avoid this sad sequence.

The student who has the most passes at the top grade has 5 A Levels and 3 S Levels. He is in the *Guinness Book of Records*. His 'secret' was:

> 'Start revising early and remember it is a lot easier to learn over a long period than trying to cram at the end.'

He also worked hard:

> 'I guess I was also very introverted then and spent two or three hours a night doing homework.'

But spaced revision was the key to his success.

FIRST YEAR

5.2 The first term of A Levels

When people start their A Levels, there is usually a spate of eager activity: books are bought; equipment is bought; effort is expended. Some of the effort is wasted on work which quite soon is seen not to have been necessary, and the intensity of work drops, not to rise again until nearing the last third of the course.

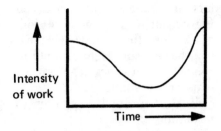

Diagram showing an *undesirable* fluctuation of effort over an A Level course

A better pattern is to have smaller fluctuations of effort over the duration of your course.

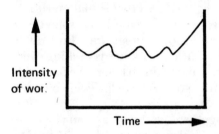

Diagram showing a *more desirable* fluctuation of effort over an A Level course

Throughout the whole of your course, always be sure you spend your time *on what is important.* Do not waste time by doing too much at the beginning and not enough in the middle of your course. Make sure you use the best books and that you deploy your time on what is really important. You need – from the outset – three things to ensure your effort is well directed: plenty of past questions; some examiners' reports on past examinations; and the syllabus. And that is probably the order of their usefulness to you. Buy these now. Use them for every topic you cover throughout your course. Always consult them before beginning any topic. You then clarify the target of your study.

5.3 Getting work done during term time

The first task is to establish your time blocks during which you will work as a habit. Habit is vital. Once something is established as a habit, it becomes easy, like eating three meals a day. It is actually two time blocks which you have to establish. The main one is to work from 7 to 9 pm each weekday evening, with 10 minutes' break in the middle. The subsidiary one is to work one other hour during each day, and to decide now exactly which hour on which day, for each weekday. This gives 15 hours during the working week. You should work at the weekend as well, for one two-hour session. Saturday morning is a good time, or failing that, Sunday evening. This gives in all 17 hours a week: that is about right as a norm, though you will go above and below this at times. The process described could be called 'landscaping' one's time.

Having established your time blocks, there are three pointers to help you get work done during term time:

1. *For written work, start early and finish early,* doing one assignment at a time. Starting early is often a problem: it is all too easy to leave beginning until too near the date on which the work has to be handed in. Procrastination rituals are undertaken . . . that is to say, there is always something which seems (mistakenly) more important. But don't procrastinate. Start early: written work needs mulling over. Equally, aim to finish early: aim to finish before the handing-in deadline. Then, if anything occurs to delay you, you have some time in hand.

   Also, focus on one assignment at a time, and stick with it until you finish it. You then feel you have made progress. Do not flit from one assignment to another, or you will be continually 'picking up the threads' of your thinking. I feel this is an extremely valuable principle.

2. *For learning work, start early and finish late.* As soon as you know you have a test, make a revision note. This is not the final revision note you will use before A Levels: it can be thrown away. It is a temporary aid but it establishes the habit of using revision notes, as well as helping you learn for the test in hand. At the beginning of each learning session, look over the entire note. Within the note, master one small 'cell' at a time. Repetitions (which usually take the form of reading over the material) should alternate with acts of recall. It is safest to look immediately if you cannot remember, to avoid implanting guesses in your mind. Learning is best done in small bursts which are spread over as long a period as possible. Thus, for learning work, start early and have short sessions spaced out right up to the time of testing.

3. *For all work, say to yourself: 'By X o'clock I will have done Y amount of work.'* Then, after a short period, see how you are getting along. Always have a target when you sit down to work: know how much you are going to achieve in a work session, otherwise you work in a drifting fashion.

5.4 Consolidating work during term time

Once your teacher has completed a unit of work in class, you should revise this. Such 'immediate revision' is immensely valuable. It clears up any difficulty while the topic is still fresh, and clarifies the material bringing it into sharp focus. You can see the topic as a whole, and viewing it in this way can shed new light. Things fall into place. The Saturday two-hour work session discussed in section 5.3 is a good time for this recapping process. You can get away with not doing this 'immediate revision'; no one will check, unless it coincides with a test. But it is wise to make post-topic recapping a matter of policy.

5.5 The Christmas holiday

During your first term you should have been doing immediate revision, that is, looking over work when it has just been covered. Tests will have encouraged you to do this. During this holiday, it is necessary to do some maintenance revision, ie go over your first term's work. It is not easy to do this during the Christmas holiday: there is Christmas; there is the New Year. But it is very important to consolidate your first term's work over the Christmas holiday. Imagine there is a big test on the first day of the spring term.

5.6 Spring term

Make sure your effort does not 'dip': remember the first diagram on p 53. One way to maintain your drive is to start thinking what you are going to do when you leave. True, you have another year of your A Levels after this one, but it soon goes and careers thinking must begin now.

5.7 Spring holiday

This is so often wasted by first year sixth formers. Of course you must consolidate your spring term's work, but the key job this holiday, once that is done, is to prepare for the end-of-year internal examinations. These examinations can be used as practice for your A Levels, and you should practise preparing. Again, pretend that you have a big test when you go back for the summer term, and get revision notes together on all your work so far. This is excellent practice in making revision notes. Usually people find it best to do a final set of revision notes beginning at Christmas in their second year, when the work can be seen with the benefit of extra maturity and experience, but these revision notes could be a guide.

You will have little time during the summer term to prepare for your end-of-year internal examinations: staff have syllabuses to cover and will not give you much revision time. Lack of preparation in the spring holidays will mean either pressure or a poor shot at your end-of-year internal exams. Easter revision is the answer. Remember the highly successful student mentioned at the beginning of this chapter.

5.8 Dealing with mid-course lack of motivation

It can happen that motivation flags during the middle of your A Level course. The freshness of the start has gone; the urgency of the end has yet to come. Interest can wane. You have to consider other sources of propulsion. They are:

1. The realisation that A Levels are a *means to a desired aim*, for example:
    (a) Getting into university.
    (b) Getting into a particular career.
    (c) Being 'a success'.
    (d) Making one's parents happy.

2. The sense of *felt achievement*.
    (a) Really understanding something is a good feeling.
    (b) Getting a unit of work done in a set time makes you feel you are achieving something.
    (c) Doing well in a test is a big boost. Work very hard for any test.

All motivation comes down to a matter of need. If your motivation flags, you must answer the question, 'Why do I need to do this?' You will not be more motivated until you have specified this answer to yourself.

5.9 Summer term

Two things: try to do about half an hour's revision a day in preparation for your end-of-year exams (make it a habit to finish off your weekday evening study times with a bit of revision); and second, firm right up on careers thinking. Neither of these things is at all burdensome, but if you don't do them they will store up trouble for you in the future.

5.10 Summer holiday

You can have a really good break in the summer – and you should, for the coming year is going to be tough! But you have some tasks for the summer holidays: consolidate and go over your year's work, concentrating on any weaknesses; do wide reading, being guided by past questions and by examiners' reports; do some preparatory work on next year's syllabus as this will make the second year much easier.

SECOND YEAR

5.11 Autumn term

The pace hots up now. Beware of getting behind with your work. Get started on it as soon as it is set, and aim to finish well ahead of the handing-in time. Do not get to the end of the term with a backlog of work, for there are always extra events towards Christmas and you will find it harder then to finish assignments. Get your applications off early, by half term at the latest (some need to go in earlier): this may increase your chances of acceptance, but in any case it decreases your anxiety and early offers will add to your motivation. If you are nervous about interviews, remember Winston Churchill's advice and imagine the interviewer is sitting in front of you in only his underpants.

5.12 The Christmas holiday

You will need to use this holiday well in order to prepare for the mock examinations in January: begin to make your final set of revision notes. Start on topics that are fully complete. The process of making final revision notes begins now and must be finished by the end of the spring holiday. You will have been referring to past questions and to examiners' reports throughout your course, but do so again now to check your coverage of a topic before making your final revision note on it. You cannot do revision notes on all your work for the mock exams, so do some quick, rough revision notes on the topics that cannot (because of lack of time or incompleteness of coverage) be finished now.

It is vital you plan your time over Christmas. People are often reluctant to do this. They make statements like: 'I can only work when I feel like it.' What they fear is the supposed limitation on freedom that they feel planning imposes. But planning saves a great deal of time in the long run: the total time to complete planned tasks is less than for unplanned tasks. And planning actually gives you more freedom: by telling you when you should be working, it also tells you when you need not be! What is needed is a simple but effective planning method.

The first thing is to '*landscape*' your time, ie decide the times of the day when you are going to work, a concept mentioned earlier. Occasionally students work to school times during the holiday, changing over subject matter when they would have changed subjects at school. This is one way, but it fragments your time, and you are better off concentrating on a topic or subject for longer than a term-time session. It is probably best to work from 10 am to 1 pm and from 7 to 9 pm, with 10-minute breaks from 50 minutes to the hour. As a generalisation, the afternoon is not such a good time to work following revision all morning, *but* there may well be people who find this their most productive time, and they should not be put off. As an alternative to the evening session, you could work from 4 to 6 pm for your second session.

The next stage is to *decide what to do when.* Having insisted on planning, one must now insist on avoiding over-planning! You need something simple and workable which will take best advantage of the holiday you have, which is very likely to be only some 14 days in total. I suggest compiling a diagram like the one opposite.

There are one of two points to remember about this diagram:

1. *Weighting.* This method enables you to consider logically whether you wish to give one A Level more time than the others.
2. *A unit a day.* You do a complete unit of one A Level on one day: do not mix subjects. Each unit is as much as you could just about do in the morning alone, if you worked really hard and things went really well. The second session of the day is overspill time – or free as a reward if you really do finish as planned, though going over your day's work before sleeping is a good idea.
3. *Ticking days.* Every day is ticked as it passes: both the free ones and the work ones. You have the flexibility to choose what to do each day. Many people find that two days on the same subject is a good idea. Ticking days is a morale booster and a motivator.

It is best to see A Levels as being one full year followed by one full term and an extended period of exam build-up lasting the other

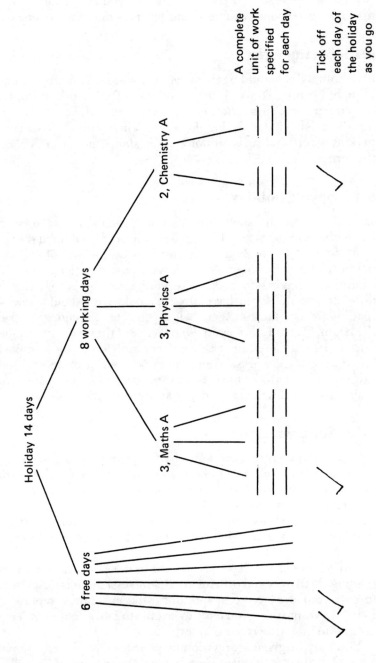

How to plan holiday work

Holiday 14 days

6 free days

8 working days

3, Maths A

3, Physics A

2, Chemistry A

A complete unit of work specified for each day

Tick off each day of the holiday as you go

two terms of the second year. This is how you could think of it: it may not correspond with how your teachers pace their courses.

5.13 Spring term

One hour a day should be given over to revision. Make it your final hour of evening study. I know you have fresh work to do, but remember the *Guinness Book of Records* student. Make time for one hour's revision a day during the week. A major aim is to carry on making your final revision notes. This should go on throughout the term.

5.14 Spring holiday

Use the same holiday time planning method you used at Christmas (see section 5.12 on p 57). This is a vital holiday. You must finish all your final revision notes by the end of it if you possibly can (remember to check with past questions and with examiners' reports to make sure your coverage is first rate in difficult areas). If you have any set books, you should now be reading them again and again: when you get to the end, go back to the beginning and start again. Knowledge of the text is much more important than anything else – and certainly much more important than critical works. Think of set books as a comprehension exercise: knowledge of the text is the most important requirement. This also includes firm memory of apposite quotations.

5.15 Summer term

You finished your revision notes by the beginning of this term (I trust) and now you have to keep going over them. Go over them again and again. Look at the note, then try to recall what is there. When you are stuck, look immediately to save sowing guesses in your mind. You must not just learn, but *over*learn your material so that you have it at your fingertips under the pressure of the exam room.

Any set books you have are treated in the same way: you keep reading them over and over again. Before sessions, it is a good idea to cast your eye over past questions and examiners' reports: A Level is gymnastics – you have to be able to move your knowledge around to fit a wide range of questions.

You may be given set revision by your teachers. There are two ways of dealing with this: either fit your own revision in with what is set, or do set work on weekdays before 7 pm, keeping weekday evenings and the weekend for your own revision. Students tend to prefer the latter policy. Also, I have noticed that many students find it a good idea to revise one A Level subject for three consecutive study sessions before changing to another.

Two don'ts. Try to avoid doing new work. You shouldn't need to anyway, but now is the time to consolidate, not to push out the boats. Second, don't cut out work, omitting to study it for the exam. Mass axing of material is the first step towards failing, and some students are tempted to 'spot' topics, and then cut out large hunks of their course. Look at it another way. Concentrate on key areas, giving them extra attention. They are bound to be on the question paper, and your smaller topics are easier to learn then because they fit into the key areas. Concentration on key areas can improve a mark by 10 per cent, but beware of leaving out material, for, apart from anything else, your teachers may have left out some of the course anyway. If you must spot (which is like gambling on the horses), do it as a fringe activity, very much as an extra 'on the side': just look over the last few papers (which is what the setter does). No elaborate statistical analyses. On the other hand, try to get some clues (from past papers and from examiners' reports) about what could turn up. Be 'cue seeking', not 'cue deaf'.

GENERAL POINTS

5.16 Sleep

I can recall a potential grade A student ending up with a grade E through lack of sleep. I walked up and down beside her in the exam room to keep her awake! Resits are a miserable experience. Clearly, making some sort of decision on sleep is a prerequisite for success.

Research suggests that it is difficult to be dogmatic about how much sleep someone needs: this (as all else in study) remains a personal decision. It is true there are 'morning' and 'evening' people when it comes to working. There is one crucial principle: everyone should ascertain by experience the amount of sleep they need to feel really good, then make sure they get it. Girls need more sleep than boys, and at 18, people need less sleep than at 16. However, an appropriate generalisation would be eight hours' sleep, from 11 pm to 7 am.

5.17 Recreation

It's a good idea to have one hour of recreation a day (a walk, a game – anything). Have Saturday afternoon and evening off. On Sunday, work as much as you need to, otherwise rest.

5.18 Managing stress

Stress can destroy you, but pressure in moderation is a spur to achievement. The flow chart on p 64 shows you how to take the anguish out of stress, which then becomes useful pressure.

5.19 Handwriting

Bad handwriting tires an examiner, and makes it hard for him to grasp your work as a whole. Checking up on, and improving, handwriting is not as hard as one might think.

Of the specimens shown opposite, (b) is easier to read than (a) because it is closer to print. Most of what we read is print, and handwriting that approximates to print is thus easier to read.

However, we are not printing machines – we cannot write exactly like print: in the specimens, (c) is the printed alphabet, and (d) is a hand-written alphabet based on it, but with a few changes to make it easier for the hand. The a, g, k and y are different, for example, and the letters tend to be oval and leaning to the right. They are grouped according to formation. The closer your handwriting is to them, the better.

It is best to concentrate on two or three letters and improve them. A friend can isolate the most important ones for you. Most difficulties arise because one letter looks like another, and improvement in two or three letters can make a big difference. If you are practising a letter, practise the whole group in which it stands.

Alternatively, it may be that one important characteristic needs attention; for example to carve out the letters more, or to write smaller (smaller writing, but not too small, is easier to read).

Legibility is greatly assisted if you ensure that letters occupy all the zones they should. For instance, 'i' is only middle zone, 'p' is middle and lower zones, and 'h' is middle and upper zones. Make sure that ascending strokes really do go up, and that descending strokes really do go down.

(a)

"The poetry of Dylan Thomas has no social reference or relevance." Discuss.

If sex, decay and death are ~~not~~ not social subjects ~~and~~ or relevant, than the above statement is true. Most people automatically think that the ~~the~~ word "social" is a synonym for "political" which, of course, it is not. However, as the term "social" in-

(b)

What part did Strafford play in the personal rule of Charles I?

Thomas Wentworth, Earl of Strafford was the greatest minister of Charles I. He belonged to an old and wealthy Yorkshire family and was educated at St. John's College, Cambridge. He entered

(c)

a b c d e f g h i j k l m n
o p q r s t u v w x y z

(d)

itl/nmrhbpk/uy/cad
gqoe/vwvw/fjs/x/z

Handwriting (see 5.19)

HOW TO SUCCEED IN A LEVELS

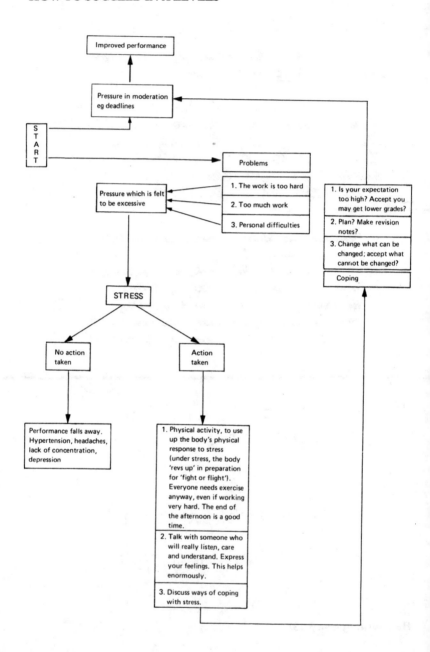

Managing stress (see 5.18)

5.20 Grammar and spelling

These sound boring. Probably your enthusiasm has already plunged at their very mention! But they are about the correct use of language, so you need proficiency in them; and if you make a collection of some useful principles, you will find that improving your work is rewarding and fun.

Ignorance of grammar can lead to comic errors, as in the incorrect version of the following pair of sentences:

Incorrect: She took the letter and, shaking her head, put it through the letter box.

Correct: She took the letter and put it through the letter box, shaking her head as she did so.

There is a useful grammatical principle here: modifying words must be clearly connected with the words they modify. Here is a less blatant example, but you will notice the extra impact of the correct version:

Incorrect: At one point, Hamlet argues that he only lacks the right moment to kill Claudius.

Correct: At one point, Hamlet argues that he lacks only the right moment to kill Claudius.

Another useful grammatical principle is: parallel parts in a sentence must be parallel in form. For example:

Incorrect: Excellent students are often precise and possess originality.

Correct: Excellent students are often precise and original.

Incorrect: English literature students are more familiar with Eliot than Pound.

Correct: English literature students are more familiar with Eliot than with Pound.

Notice how parallelism increases clarity.

A stimulating book to make you think about your grammar is: Waldhorn, A and Zeiger, A (1979) *English Made Simple*, London: W H Allen. Look at section two on sentence errors, and at section seven on style. Do the exercises, study the solutions given, and then read as much of the explanation as you need.

A perceptive and sensitive book for improving your style is: Thomson, O M (1982) *A Matter of Style*, London: Hutchinson. It is intended principally for A Level English literature students, but it is of value to any A Level student.

HOW TO SUCCEED IN A LEVELS

Incorrect spelling undermines the quality of your work. Being able to spell correctly all the words you need boosts confidence and provides satisfaction. There is an excellent short section on spelling at the back of: Ridout, R (1980) *The Pan Spelling Dictionary*, London: Pan Books. Ridout does more than provide rules: he provides principles and explanations, so that you understand and remember tricky spellings.

Chapter 6

The Examination

When the examination itself arrives, your careful preparation along the lines discussed will give you a firm basis of confidence. However, there are certain points to remember so that you ensure all your hard work gains its reward.

6.1 Relevance

More people under-achieve or fail by not answering the question than for any other single reason.

Irrelevance can arise from *misunderstanding* the question, and marks are given only for what happens to be relevant by chance as it were.

The question can also be *disregarded* (in spite of having been understood at the outset) by the examinee ignoring it or by making a token gesture towards it at the beginning or the end. In such situations some observations can have relevance, and be worth a few marks.

Partial irrelevance is also common, by examinees beginning on the question and then wandering off it, or by beginning in a confused way and then working towards the question as the essay progresses. That which is relevant is credited: that which is not, is not.

Another error is to *twist* the question to fit a prepared line of thought. This receives a mark according to what is relevant and what is not, and the mark will be considerably lower than what could have been achieved by answering the question as set.

Examples of irrelevance in answer to two essay titles on an
A Level General Studies paper

What are the advantages and disadvantages of Sixth Form Colleges?
  Many candidates wrote about sixth form education in general.

Do you feel yourself to be a European?
  Many candidates wrote on the history of the Common Market.

Ways of being irrelevant

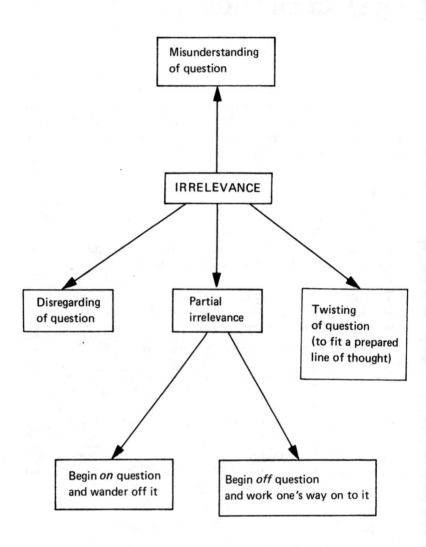

In every examination, you must answer the question, the whole question, dealing with the issues it raises, but not going beyond that.

6.2 Tackling the paper

In tackling the paper, there are four key points to remember:

1. *Choose the questions very carefully.* This is a crucial and much neglected art: you can ruin your whole A Level by choosing the wrong questions. Take your time and weigh your choice very carefully, making sure you follow the instructions on the paper. Often, after an exam, the teacher thinks students will have chosen, say, questions 1, 3 and 5; then he finds they have chosen 2, 4 and 6 – in view of their studies, he is amazed! This is an indication of how common it is for the wrong questions to be chosen.

2. *Tackle the easiest question first.* This will not always be the compulsory question. In this way you write yourself in and give yourself confidence. You are also thinking unconsciously about the harder questions as you write. Move up the order of difficulty.

3. *Divide your time carefully between the questions.* This, like the other two points, is not spectacular knowledge, but like anything else in life, success comes to those who do the basics well. You will see from the table on p 70 that an average of 10 on each of four essays gives an E grade, whereas an average of 16 on each of four essays gives a B grade. This table is worth studying carefully.

4. *Check over your paper at the end.* Make sure you are saying what you intended to say. Weed out any errors. Any crossing out should be with a single horizontal line. Evaluation of your work is an important part of the creative process.

6.3 Writing essays in the exam room

The fundamentals which were discussed earlier still hold good, but there are slight modifications, given that this is an examination. Writing an essay in an exam is a three-stage process:

1. *React to the question.* Look at the key words in the question and they will trigger ideas, which you then list in rough. More ideas can be generated by asking yourself questions about the question: your answers to yourself will become rough

HOW TO SUCCEED IN A LEVELS

Table showing marks related to A Level grades, indicating the importance of dividing time carefully between questions

Percentage marks	A Level grade
70 and above	A
61–69	B
54–60	C
47–53	D
40–46	E
33–39	N
32 and below	U (or F)

Note.

4 answers at

16 each give 64 per cent, a grade B
14 each give 56 per cent, a grade C
12 each give 48 per cent, a grade D
10 each give 40 per cent, a grade E

(Each answer out of 25.)

notes. Beware in particular the exact meaning of the following words:

Analyse. Break down complex issues, ideas and processes into component parts and recognise how the various parts are related.
Compare. Point out similarities or likenesses between things. In practice, this may also involve pointing out the contrasts or differences.
Discuss. Explain clearly several sides of a topic.
Evaluate. Give a judgement or opinion as to the worth of something. Judgements should be reasoned and supported by arguments or facts. This is not the same as describe.

Stage 1, then, involves listing ideas as they come to you by free association. Always jot down ideas the moment they come into your head. Evidence (eg examples and quotations) is particularly important.

2. *Structure your reactions.* The next stage is to structure your reactions by forming paragraphs. This is often not done, and ideas are simply put down in their free association format. However, diffuse and rambling answers can never score high marks, even when the material is good; conversely, a structured answer tends to gain marks even when its content is comparatively thin. The desired structure of an exam essay is shown in the following diagram.

The structure of an exam essay

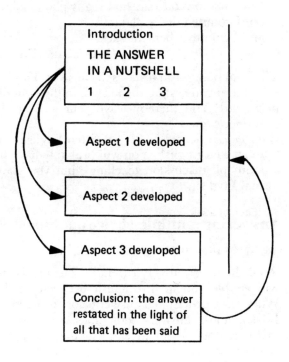

The answer is given in nutshell form in the first paragraph, and the three major aspects of the answer are touched upon. This helps to ensure relevance, and it also informs the examiner of your general line (a great help). Each aspect will have a paragraph to itself, giving three major paragraphs (and each paragraph could have three key ideas in it). You do not have to keep rigidly to the number three, but an essay develops force in this way, and it is notable that many sayings which stay in the mind are three-part lists:

> Government of the people,
> by the people,
> for the people.
>
> (Abraham Lincoln, 1863)

> Never in the field of human conflict
> has so much been owed
> by so many
> to so few.
>
> (Winston Churchill, 1940)

> I'm not allowed to say how many planes joined the raid,
> but I counted them all out
> and I counted them all back.
>
> (Brian Hanrahan, HMS *Hermes*, 1982)

The final paragraph restates the answer. This is not a simple repetition: you restate the answer in the light of all that has been said. You thereby leave your answer clearly in the examiner's mind.

3. *Write in good written English.* Written English is more formal than spoken English. You will probably have had a certain amount of 'discussion teaching', but you should write in formal English.

6.4 Answering multiple-choice questions

One suggested procedure is:

1. Read the question very carefully. The precise words it uses will enable you to distinguish between possible answers. Work out a provisional answer before proceeding.
2. Look at all the answers: sometimes a seemingly right answer (a distractor) is put in early in the list, with the correct answer coming later.
3. Eliminate the answers that are wrong. This should leave you with about two possibles.
4. Discriminate between the two. Both may have some truth in them but one will be closer than the other.
5. At the end, make an attempt at questions that you have left out. These attempts can often be right.
6. When you have finished, check over your answers. People can be reluctant to do this, especially with multiple choice, but corrections made at the end are often good ones because you have done the whole paper and are thus 'well oiled'.

6.5 The examiner's task

An A Level examiner will have about 160 papers to mark in four weeks. This means 40 a week, or about 6 every single day. He will also, more often than not, have his ordinary job to do. Your paper will be marked in about 15 to 20 minutes. It is therefore clear that all the ways in which you can help the examiner will tend to dispose him favourably towards your paper. So number the questions in the same way as on the question paper; organise your work sensibly; assemble your answer sheets in the right order. Make life as easy as possible for the examiner.

Chapter 7

The Psychology of Study

The ideas and content of this book are presented in such a way that you can use them, but they are underpinned by a psychological base. It is interesting to examine this base separately, as it will further reinforce what has been said.

7.1 Motivation

1. *Goal setting.* People exert themselves more when a target has been set. The target must be realistic, though. Thus, when you sit down to work, you should have a target amount that you wish to complete in a given time, preferably a complete unit of work. You therefore feel a *compulsion* to finish it, and a sense of *achievement* when you have done so. You need a specific and clearly defined objective.
2. *Abolishing procrastination rituals.* It can be very difficult to start a task. This is often a problem with painters who are unable to start work on a blank canvas. 'Jump into the water' by starting punctually at the allotted time.
3. *Concentration* is intense attention. You have to 'park' your mind on the task by trying to pick out the important *details*. The greater your concentration, the more effective your learning.
4. *Competition.* This can be a motivator. Co-operation can be a bigger one. Discussion with a fellow student or mutual testing can be a big bonus. More use could be made of collaborative learning. Work out between you other ways in which it can be done. However, both of you must know the material quite well to collaborate really fruitfully.
5. *Modelling.* It can help to model yourself on good students. For example, when do good students start to revise (this was discussed); what sort of revision notes do they make? Think carefully about what the really good students in your group do.
6. *Habit.* Effectiveness in any sphere requires habit. It is an *automatic* response as a result of repetition; for this reason, it is

a powerful force to have on your side, eg work from 7 to 9 pm each weekday evening; or always jot down ideas for an essay at the moment they come into your head. You need to exercise judgement, though: unreflective habit can also constrain learning, eg habitually reading in one way, unaware of scanning or skimming.

7. *Interest* is a strong motivator. You can increase your interest by *having views* on what you are studying. You then become emotionally involved in your work. Also, as far as possible, choose books which put points in an interesting way. If you don't like one book, have the confidence to reject it and find another.

8. *Self-questioning*. The constant posing of questions to yourself generates activity. By simply asking yourself questions, you feel urged to find the answers: 'How does this work?'; 'What does this word mean?'; 'Why was this policy adopted?'. You can sense a pull to action.

9. *Self-concept*. Try to work out in your mind a picture of the sort of person you want to be. You'll then tend to become that.

7.2 Thinking

There are four main types of thinking:

1. *Logical thinking*, which means reasoning. In its narrow sense it involves drawing conclusions from facts, as in Mathematics. More widely, it involves activities such as arriving at a general statement on the basis of particular instances, and trying to prove or disprove arguments, as in arts subjects.

2. *Creative thinking* means perceiving new relationships between facts and ideas. This comes into essay writing, for example. Its stages are:

   (a) Preparation   – you gather your material.
   (b) Incubation   – you let the material and the question simmer in the unconscious (hence the need to start essays early).
   (c) Illumination   – you allow ideas to emerge into consciousness.
   (d) Elaboration   – you communicate your ideas on paper.
   (e) Evaluation   – you check over what you have written to see whether it says what you intended it to say. You criticise, modify and improve.

3. *Lateral thinking* is a type of creative thinking identified by Edward de Bono. Problems are solved by rejecting the ordinary way of looking at them, and choosing an entirely different way. Here is an example: it is a trick from a trick shop which requires lateral thinking in order to find a solution. You have to get both balls into the cupped shelves at each end of the container.

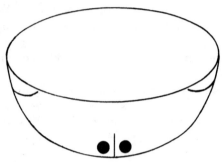

The ordinary way of trying to do this would be to tilt the plastic container – but as you try to get the second ball in, the first one falls out! The lateral thinking solution is to spin the container, so that both balls go into their holes simultaneously by centrifugal force. This type of thinking is fun, but not much used in A Level, except in the context of creative thinking.

4. *Intuitive thinking.* This is where a small amount of information is given and you make an intuitive leap to a solution. Again, this is not much used in A Level except in the context of creative thinking.

7.3 Memory

With attention, material passes into short-term memory (STM). This is a type of echo box. STM holds material for up to 30 seconds, remembering it by sound, eg a telephone number which you have looked up can be remembered by repeating it (which is what people do). STM can remember about seven items, and is easily disrupted: for instance, the telephone number will slip out of your mind if someone disturbs you, though if you are not disturbed, the retrieval of the information is error-free. However, STM cannot improve its performance above about seven items, although 'chunking' helps, as when the telephone operator gives you the number in pairs or chunks, as follows:

four figure number	24/68
five figure number	24/685
six figure number	24/68/57

Long-term memory (LTM) is different. It is a type of filing cabinet. It can hold material from minutes to decades, and it remembers by analysis. Its capacity is unlimited and it is less easily disrupted than STM, though retrieval is more error-prone. It can, however, improve, as follows.

Material is transferred from STM to LTM by thinking about it, repeating it and using it. This transfer is achieved by: analysing; understanding; discussion; exercises; answering past questions; self-testing; making diagrams; and compiling revision notes.

Retrieval from LTM is best accomplished by putting questions to yourself. Searching then takes place and recall develops by free association (ie letting one idea lead to another). Free association is an important technique in tackling exam essays; here is an example:

Free association to recall the name of a student who left four years ago.

She had brown eyes.
She was tall.
She played hockey.
She was friends with Wendy.
She told good jokes.
She became a dentist.
Her name was *SOPHIE*.

Key words in revision notes act as cues to help retrieval.

Forgetting is a real threat, and happens because of retroactive inhibition (ie later knowledge buries old knowledge), and because of fading, though more the former than the latter. Poor concentration, poor understanding and high anxiety also contribute.

7.4 Approaches to learning

There are two main approaches to learning:

1. *Rote learning*. This is learning by heart, or learning 'parrot fashion'. It has a place in A Level work (eg in learning quotations for English) but its place is limited, because A Level is not simply the reproduction of knowledge.
2. *Learning by understanding*. This is the key learning approach to all A Level work. It is the central aim of your effort.

7.5 Ways of learning

Some key learning principles are:

1. *Activity*. Learning is an active process. Do not passively sit and read notes and books: *actively* try to recall what is there; think about past questions; organise material. Have opinions in class, and state them.

2. *Organisation of material*. Gestalt psychologists believe that the mind actively tries to organise what is experienced into a meaningful pattern, or construction. Parts which do not seem to fit may be discarded.

   Good students assist the mind's attempts to structure knowledge by structuring it themselves, trying to fit details into a wider whole. Hence, for an essay, read something short first to gain an overview. Before reading a chapter of a detailed book, it is a good idea to try to appraise the chapter as a whole by looking over the headings and subheadings. When making a revision note, try to put a whole topic (or a whole aspect of a topic) on one side.

   When learning something, it should first be read through entirely to get the general drift. Then break it down into as small 'wholes' as possible in order to achieve errorless learning. Learn them by repeating them and trying to recall them, perfecting one at a time. Repetitions should alternate with acts of recall. It is safest to look immediately when you cannot remember, to avoid implanting guesses in your mind. Repetition usually takes the form of reading over the material.

3. *Spaced repetition*. Periods of repetition-and-recall should be relatively brief (perhaps 15 minutes), and well distributed. The intervals give the material time to sink in. Hence, start memory work early for tests, instead of concentrating into one sitting all the time that can be given to the particular task. If you end up having only one evening, try to repeat-and-recall periodically between 7 and 9 pm.

4. *Retroactive inhibition*. This is interference with the memory of one set of material caused by the learning of another set: later learning covers up earlier memories. Learning before you go to bed, say at the end of your 7 to 9 study period, is a good idea so long as you are not too tired, because retroactive inhibition is avoided. Learning before you go to bed is advantageous because there is a lack of later learning, as sleep follows, though it will inhibit learning which has taken

place earlier in the day. Perhaps it is best done as a review of the day's work. Learning deep into the night is different though, and not a good idea: attention fades, and fatigue follows the next day.

5. *Review*. One calls this revision. There are three types:

   (a) *Immediate revision* (review just after you have been taught the material);
   (b) *Maintenance revision* (review between learning and testing for the final time);
   (c) *Terminal revision* (review just before final testing).

All are important. Their order of effectiveness is: terminal, immediate, maintenance.

Repetition of material during each of the three types of review is important, as repetition is a vital learning principle.

6. *Overlearning*. Forgetting is an enormous problem. Details slip away very quickly. So long as you can understand the material initially, details can be brushed up by revision notes, but the rapidity of forgetting is one reason why revision is so much emphasised in this book. It is important to *overlearn*. Overlearning means the continued revision of material even when it seems to be known perfectly, eg going over revision notes again and again. Overlearning is a protection against anxiety-caused forgetting in the exam room.

7. *Recency*. The best remembered items are those most recently experienced. Hence, revision notes should be gone over right up to the last minute before the exam. Being short, they are an ideal way of using the principle of recency.

8. *Knowledge of results*. You can use the principle on yourself by assessing how you are getting on in achieving the work target of each session. Tell yourself 'how you are doing'. You may say to yourself: 'I must work more quickly to meet my target', or 'I'm doing well tonight – I must keep it up.' Check that you remember each small chunk of work before you go on to the next one.

9. *Reinforcement*. When you perform an act of desired behaviour, you reinforce it by rewarding yourself. You will recognise this concept at work in the comments on the use of time during the Christmas holiday of the second year, and you'll probably remember receiving 'merit marks' as a child, at primary school. The reinforcement should come immediately after the desired behaviour, eg having a coffee

straight after completing a unit of work. The concept is used more loosely in the discussion on how to increase mid-course motivation.

7.6 The SQ3R method

One method of reading and note making, which was created to combine all the important psychological principles of study, is the SQ3R method of F P Robinson, from Ohio State University. It has found its way into many study books in a diluted form. It is given here briefly but in its original form.

1. *Survey*. 1 minute. Look at the headings and final summary of the chapter.
2. *Question*. Turn the first heading into a question.
3. *Read*. Read the whole section to find the answer to the question.
4. *Recite*. Compile 'working notes' as follows:

   (a) Work from memory, but peek if you have to.
   (b) Write down the heading.
   (c) Note key words and phrases, with examples.
   (d) Use your own words where possible.
   (e) Be brief.

   Stages two, three and four are repeated with all the remaining sections of the chapter.
5. *Review*. 5 minutes. Look at the overall layout of your note and then test yourself by covering up points, recalling and checking.

This method is very effective for mastering a textbook, but you cannot combine material from different books into one note. Robinson's work is stimulating, and can be followed up in: Robinson, F P (1970) *Effective Study*, New York: Harper & Row.

Chapter 8

Coursework

Coursework is any activity which you carry out during your course and which is directly assessed as part of the actual examination. A number of A Levels and AS Levels now include coursework. The range of coursework is wide, from fieldwork and experimental laboratory work, to individual studies and collections of pieces of written work.

8.1 Three golden rules

In all coursework, you should:

1. Make sure you have the *precise details* from the examination board of what is required. These days, such details are freely available. Your teachers will have them. Ask. The comments in this chapter will be widely applicable, but should be tailored to the requirements of each piece of coursework, as stated by the board.
2. Learn from the *experience of others*. Seek the views of past students or of students in the year above you. Ask your teachers about the errors and strengths of previous coursework similar to yours.
3. *Start writing-up early*. At least a quarter of the time for a project should be allocated to drafting and amending the final version. This means you must begin work on your project as soon as it is set, to allow time for mulling it over and amending it at the end. It helps to do some writing up as you go along, if you can.

8.2 Choosing a topic

1. *A good topic interests you and the reader*. Your topic must provide you with sufficient interest to sustain long study, otherwise choose something else. But in addition, you must make your topic interesting for the reader. Surface devices like violence, catastrophe or the unmasking of a hero create interest, as

does on a deeper level any topic which shows that something is not what it seems. The interesting is mid-way between the absurd and the obvious.

2. *The size must be right.* Beware too broad a topic. It is better to write a lot about a little, than a little about a lot. Narrow down your topic. For example:

> The nuclear issue.
> Nuclear power, not weapons.
> The safety of nuclear power.
> Has Chernobyl had an impact on the development of safe nuclear power in the United Kingdom?

Be sure that the topic is not so narrow as to leave you with too few sources. This angle needs checking before you start.

3. *Questions make the best titles.* Your title must centre on a problem, preferably expressed as a question. Your choice of title is crucial in spurring you on to show what you can do. A problem expressed as a question gives you direction and purpose: you select, arrange and interpret material, rather than simply accumulate it. A problem that cannot be turned into a question is not a problem at all. The title 'Women in the novels of D.H. Lawrence' is not likely to produce as good a result as 'Does "O for a life of sensations rather than thoughts" truly reflect the nature of Keats's poetry?'

the 2 main points are efficiently organ

8.3 Doing the research

Categorize Note Cards if poss.
Main topic at top + sub
numbered then underlined se
pages 98-5

1. *Collecting material.* Read short, general material first, to acquire a feel for your topic, then move to longer, more detailed material. Start with modern books first, then use older ones as necessary. Sources can be recorded on (3 × 5) inch cards, and notes on 5 × 8 inch cards. In both cases, use only one side of each card; you can then easily move material around. Study the diagram on p 83 which gives examples of source and note cards.

smaller excerpts + bonnotes or paraphrased notes can go on cards for longer

2. *Representing information.* Don't forget annotated diagrams (discussed on p 31). Photographs could be useful in some cases. Graphs, bar charts and tables are the most effective ways of presenting numerical data. It is easy to under-perform on them, hence they are revised on pp 84–7. Some of the points may seem basic, but they are often not done.

excerp

from books should be paper clipped.

Examples of source and note cards used for collecting material for projects

Source cards

A book

Jung C G (1940).

The Integration of the Personality.
London: Routledge and Kegan Paul.

An article in a book

Jacobs M (1984).

"Psychodynamic Therapy: the Freudian Approach".

In Dryden W (ed);
Individual Therapy in Britain.
London: Harper and Row.

An article in a journal

Jensen A R (1969).

"How much can we boost IQ and scholastic achievement?"

Harvard Educational Review, 39, p. 1 - 123

An article in a newspaper

Buxton N (1988).

"Into Africa with Jung".

Sunday Telegraph,
17 April,
p.39

An interview

Jones M J (1988).

Jungian analyst.

Interviewed 2 January.

(handwritten notes in left margin)
...mation
– ways to
organise as
...ctly as possible
...thout ~~leaving~~
...aving out
...portant & essential
...formation

Note card

DREAMS: WATER SYMBOLISM

Jung (1940), p.67

HOW TO SUCCEED IN A LEVELS

How to draw a good graph

Graphs are used to *illustrate a trend*.
Follow the instructions and look at the example opposite.

1. Use a sharp pencil.

2. Use graph paper.

3. Write the title of the graph.

4. Make a grid of the data.

5. Draw two axes at right angles to each other. Label the origin (the point at which they meet) 'O' and put arrows on the ends of the axes.

6. Label each axis, and state the units near each label. Performance goes on the vertical axis.

7. Choose a suitable scale to use as much of the graph paper as possible. If there is a break in the scale on either axis, indicate it as follows:

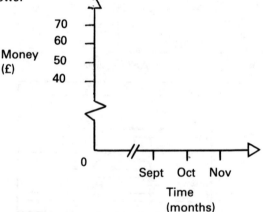

How to show breaks in the scales of a graph

8. Plot each point with a dot in a circle: ⊙

9. Join the points with straight lines if the data is *not* continuous (eg airline fatalities per month). Use a curved line if the data *is* continuous (eg changes in room temperature).

10. Add the source at the bottom.

84

COURSEWORK

An example of a good graph

Graph showing the baby's weight from birth to six weeks

Age (weeks)	birth	1	2	3	4	5	6
Weight (kgs)	3.1	2.9	2.9	3.0	3.1	3.3	3.5

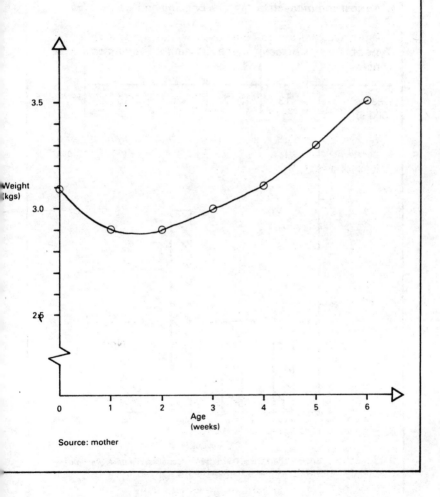

Source: mother

85

HOW TO SUCCEED IN A LEVELS

How to draw a good bar chart

Bar charts *compare separate items.*
They are constructed similarly to graphs, but note that the axes do not have arrows.
When drawing the bars, make them all the same width (4mm); keep them apart; and draw diagonal lines across them.

An example of a good bar chart

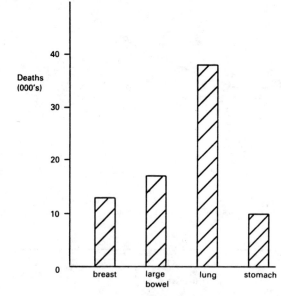

The most common lethal cancers, England and Wales, 1984

Type of cancer	breast	large bowel	lung	stomach
Deaths (000's)	13	17	38	10

Source: figures from Doll, R (1986) *Possibilities for the Prevention of Cancer*, London: The Royal Society.

How to make a good table

Tables show how a particular total is *divided up*.
Use the one below as a model. Ensure that the table develops down, not across, the page.

An example of a good table

Motorists breath-tested during a two-week police campaign in Sussex, Christmas 1985

Alcohol consumed	Number
Over the legal limit	220
Up to the legal limit	455
None	325
Total	1,000

Source: figures from local press

8.4 Writing up your study

1. *The title page.* See p 88 for a model, based on an imaginary case. A professional title page creates an excellent first impression.
2. *The contents page.* A simple layout is best, like the one on p 89. You should give the number and title of chapters, followed by their page numbers.
3. *List of illustrations.* All tables, maps and diagrams used in the study should be listed, with page numbers given.
4. *Introduction.* In this you should:

   (a) Explain why the problem is important.
   (b) State the aims of the study.
   (c) Discuss the methods of enquiry adopted.
   (d) Acknowledge help received, eg from librarians.

An example of a title page

HOW FAR DID THE SECOND WORLD WAR AFFECT

DAILY LIFE IN EASTBOURNE?

by
Katherine Rachel Maya

A dissertation
submitted in partial fulfilment
of the requirements for A Level History
Joint Matriculation Board
June, 1988

An example of a contents page

CONTENTS

1. List of illustrations   4

2. Introduction   6

3. The Initial Impact   8

4. The Normal Pattern   12

5. Some Problem Areas   16

6. Long-term Effects.   20

7. Conclusion   24

8. Bibliography   26

5. *The main chapters.* A4 wide-lined paper is a good size, or you can type on unlined A4 paper. A well-presented hand-written report receives no less credit, but it can be helpful if you type it.

   Special references to, or quotations from, books, articles or interviews should be cited, but do not cite general or background reading. Cite sparingly, using the following examples as a guide:

   > Jung (1940) describes . . .
   > In her short study, Fordham (1959) discusses . . .
   > In Brown's standard work on the post-Freudians (Brown, 1964) . . .
   > Gross (1987, p 681) states that . . .
   > In interview, Jones (1988) argued that . . .

   Aim to keep within the word limit with a little to spare. If your study is too short, you probably haven't made, or critically developed, sufficient points; if it is too long, you have probably accumulated unnecessary material which you can edit out.

   Once you have done your first draft, put it aside for a day or so, then look at it afresh. Check not only the content, but also the English. Cross out unnecessary words. Eliminate vague subjects like 'it' or 'this'. Shorten long sentences or put in a comma so that the reader can draw breath. Read your project aloud to catch remaining errors in style.

   Remember to number the pages.

   Look out for a suitable soft-covered binder.
6. *Conclusion.* A general summary of what was found.
7. *Bibliography.* All interviews and texts actually cited should be listed in alphabetical order of author, exactly as on your source cards, models of which are on p 83. For example: Jung, C G (1940) *The Integration of the Personality*, London: Routledge and Kegan Paul.

8.5 Experiments

Some points to watch in experiments are:

1. *Design.* In deciding on the procedure to be followed, consider at least two valid alternatives, then select the best.
2. *Apparatus.* You must develop the confidence to set up equipment unaided. Consciously plan for safety. Indicate in your report the safety measures taken.

3. *Measurement and observation.* Skill in making observations is of fundamental importance: watch for instrument errors, repeat observations and acquire a reasonable range of observations, recording them in a neat and organised manner.

4. *Handling data.* Assess the reliability of your conclusions: estimate the source and size of errors in observing and processing data. Critically appraise your work: identify where something went wrong or could have been done better.

Chapter 9

Courses and Careers

This chapter looks at some of the wider considerations relating to success at A Level. But do consult your school, college or local authority careers adviser. Qualification requirements are now in a state of change. Checking is vital.

9.1 Picking the right A Levels, AS Levels and extra GCSEs

1. Check your GCSE qualifications against possible future courses at university or polytechnic and against possible future careers. If you can, use university prospectuses and literature from the organisations involved, rather than all-embracing careers guides. However, there is one guide that is indispensable; it is both detailed, clear and reliable. It is almost worth having your own copy: *University Entrance: The Official Guide*, obtainable from Sheed and Ward Ltd, 2 Creechurch Lane, London EC3A 2AQ. It tells you about all qualifications for university. If you need to pick up a GCSE or two in the sixth form, now is the time to find out. In GCSE re-takes, don't be lulled into a sense of security if the paper seems easy: you have to complete a good deal of it successfully to score a high grade. Remember you need a grade C or above if your GCSE is to count in the eyes of universities and professional bodies. It is crucial, therefore, to finish the paper and to split your effort strictly according to the marks allocated for each question. If you are not told the mark distribution, you must estimate it. In addition, it is as well to remember:

   (a) English GCSE is vital.
   (b) Oxford, Cambridge, Exeter, Warwick, Sussex and Keele universities require Maths GCSE (or a science subject at GCSE) for all entrants. If you have no Maths GCSE, you restrict your degree choice in Geography, Agriculture, Social Science, Psychology, Environmental Science and Biology. GCSE Maths is important for most jobs and courses.

(c) Oxford and Cambridge require a foreign language GCSE for entry to any of their degree courses. Lack of a foreign language at GCSE would restrict degree course choice in English and History.

(d) Check your science GCSE situation. If you are interested in science as a career, it has traditionally been wise to have studied Physics, Chemistry and Biology as separate examination subjects up to the end of the fifth form. Note, too, that beauty therapy and home economics courses need a science at GCSE. However, many schools now run only a GCSE double award science subject, incorporating the three sciences. This is likely to suffice, but do check. Here are two examples to illustrate the increasingly varied patterns of requirements:

Medicine can be entered with Chemistry A Level, plus two other A Levels from Biology, Physics and Maths, with the missing subject passed at GCSE. However, all medical schools in England, Wales and Northern Ireland will accept two AS Levels in place of a third A Level, though Chemistry A Level is still required (AS Levels are discussed later in this chapter). Details of the incorporation of AS Levels into medical school requirements vary from one medical school to another, and you should check in *University Entrance: The Official Guide* and in medical schools' prospectuses, or by writing direct to them. The United Medical and Dental Schools of Guy's and St Thomas's Hospitals, typically of the University of London's medical schools, will consider two A Levels plus two AS Levels, with the following constraints:

   (i) You must have Chemistry A Level.
  (ii) If your other A Level is a *science*, then the two AS Levels can be in any approved subjects; if your other A Level is a *non-science*, then the two AS Levels must be in science ('science' here means science and Maths).
 (iii) Some study of the three sciences up to at least GCSE level is required, but this requirement can be satisfied by a GCSE double award science covering the three sciences.

Physiotherapy requires, as a minimum, five GCSEs and two A Levels. The package must include two science subjects. Biology should be at A Level. The other A Level should preferably be a science, otherwise the second science must be at GCSE. Physics is preferable to Chemistry as the second science. A GCSE double award science is acceptable as the second science, but a single subject science is preferred. AS Levels have not been incorporated into the minimum entry requirements as stated above, but two AS Levels would be acceptable as equivalent to a third A Level. In the past, most successful applicants have had single subject 16+ passes in Biology, Physics and Chemistry before beginning A Levels, and at A Level have tended to offer three subjects, often three science A Levels. Would-be doctors have tended to fall back on Physiotherapy and Occupational Therapy.

2. Choose your A Levels on the basis of what you are good at, in a good combination, looking at traditional patterns first.

A Level Maths is a very important subject. Apart from being important in its own right, it comes into and helps Physics and Chemistry. As an example, all universities offering Chemistry degrees like A Level Maths. If you wish to take a Maths degree, two Maths subjects at A Level are a help, but if you take only one Maths subject, it must be Pure.

A Level Chemistry is a very important science. It is the science you can least afford to drop. It is also the most representative of the sciences, being both descriptive and analytic (Biology is descriptive; Physics is analytic). It helps Biology A Level.

Thus we get only two ideal science combinations at A Level.

Maths, Chemistry and Physics
The Maths helps both the Chemistry and the Physics. This is the best combination of any A Levels. Very few science-orientated careers are excluded.

Maths, Chemistry and Biology
The Maths helps the Chemistry, and the Chemistry helps the Biology. This is the other ideal combination, although rather more careers are normally excluded with this combination than with the previous combination, eg engineering.

Another two science combinations are often studied

Biology, Physics and Chemistry
This is possible, but you haven't the Maths to help the Physics and Chemistry, and you cut out careers dependent on Maths such as engineering, physics and statistics.

Biology with two arts A Levels
Science degrees are closed, but if you have a supporting science at GCSE, you can aim for paramedical careers like physiotherapy, though this will not be easy. However, Biology is harder without Chemistry, and Chemistry needs Maths, so this is not an ideal combination.

Finally, one can look at other combinations of A Levels, ie arts A Levels

Science careers are shut, but many others are open, eg accountancy, hotel and catering.

Hold on to Maths, and take it as an A Level if you can, combining it with arts subjects. It doesn't need sciences with it: it stands alone, and you will find it of value. It goes well with Economics and Geography (or with Physics and Geography, if your Physics will stand it).

Be cautious about Art, Music, Home Economics and General Studies A Levels. They are valuable subjects but are sometimes regarded askance. Look at other subjects first. Unless there is a special reason to the contrary, these are safest seen as third choice if you are short.

Try to choose a good combination, eg History, Geography and Economics; or History, English and a modern language. History, English and Geography are often done as a trio, but the load of reading is heavy. There is much to be said for choosing compatible subjects.

3. Now give full but cautious consideration to AS Levels.
    The traditional sixth form curriculum of three A Levels is

Note
The newer A Levels such as Accounting, Computer Science (or Computer Studies), Electronics and Law are also best seen as third A Levels. Prospective undergraduates in these subjects are never required to have them at A Level; other subjects are preferred.

There is a lot to be said for keeping to the standard academic school subjects for A Level. On the science side: Maths, Chemistry, Physics and Biology. On the arts side: English, History, Geography and foreign languages (though Maths is good if you can, particularly for degree courses in Geography).

more specialised than almost anywhere in the world. AS Levels are to encourage its broadening, as 75 per cent of people now at school will change their *type* of job three times in their lifetime. There is also a growing trend towards mixing A Levels, accounting for 30 per cent of all A Level students in 1985, so bridging the arts–science divide. This is a time of transition. New patterns are emerging.

AS Levels are Advanced Supplementary Levels. They are half the workload and study time of an A Level, but for that half are intellectually as demanding. Some are based on A Levels with the content reduced; others are new. AS Levels can complement A Levels if they are in the same broad subject area. They can also contrast with A Levels if they are in a different subject area, so A Level scientists can keep a foreign language, and A Level arts students can keep Maths, for instance.

For their general entry requirement, no university insists on three A Levels as a minimum. Most universities require two A Levels as a minimum, but are happy to accept two AS Levels as equal to a third A Level. Some universities will accept one A Level plus two AS Levels as a minimum, and some will accept four AS Levels as a minimum. For Oxford, the A Level minimum requirement can be met by two A Levels, by one A Level plus two AS Levels, or by four AS Levels, though Cambridge still requires at A Level a minimum of two subjects. Minimum is the operative word!

As a course requirement, universities often mention specific A Levels which you must have. AS Levels are likely to be increasingly accepted in place of named A Levels for entry to particular courses, but this is not so yet, at any rate on a large scale.

Some universities wish to see AS Levels made compulsory, and eventually may give preference to students who have taken AS Levels. But in general universities are happy with the gradual and cautious introduction of AS Levels, coupling this with a movement away from rigid entry requirements for degree courses.

Three factors may hinder the introduction of AS Levels. First, some schools may not offer them. Second, some university selectors may react coolly to them. Third, some students may not like the idea of achieving, say, a B grade in each of two AS Levels, in order to equate with a B grade in one A Level.

Be sure to consult *University Entrance: The Official Guide* on the acceptability of AS Levels as they apply to you.

A number of possible permutations of A Levels and AS Levels have, therefore, arisen:

(a) *Three A Levels.* This is the traditional package: and there is safety in tradition. You will not be disadvantaged in any way (at least for the present) by omitting to choose AS Levels.

(b) *Three A Levels plus two AS Levels.* This is like taking four A Levels, a heavy load. For the sake of breadth, you run the risk of sacrificing high grades. Two AS Levels are more usually taken in place of an A Level.

(c) *Three A Levels plus one AS Level.* You have the solidity of the traditional package coupled with the width of an AS Level, especially if it is in a contrasting subject. In a way, the best of both worlds! The AS Level could be in a complementary subject as an alternative: you could thus continue with Maths, Physics, Chemistry and Biology.

(d) *Two A Levels plus two AS Levels.* The universities are happy with this combination, and like the idea of the gradual introduction of AS Levels. But remember you will have to do well in four subjects instead of in three; and bear in mind that certain A Levels may be specified as course requirements for some courses.

(e) *Two A Levels plus one AS Level.* A good idea for the less strong candidate, but universities are likely to look for the other AS Level in practice, especially where there is competition for places. However, this combination is perfectly acceptable for entering polytechnic and for entering other careers post-A Level.

(f) *One A Level plus four AS Levels.* An unusual combination at present.

(g) *Six AS Levels.* Markedly unusual at present.

(h) *Four AS Levels.* Technically this satisfies the minimum general requirement at A Level for entry to CNAA degrees in polytechnics, and for entry to some universities. However, remember that certain A Levels will be specified in some course requirements.

9.2 What to do after A Levels

As early as the spring term of your first year in the sixth form you need to be thinking about this. Clarify in your own mind the deadlines for submitting forms. Some will need to go in during the summer term, though generally forms can go off in the first half of the autumn term of your second year in the sixth.

There are two main options: either a course (some sort of training) or employment. The way to decide what to do is to list carefully the realistic alternatives, and evaluate them. This will almost certainly involve discussions with an adviser in your school or college. Look again at the discussion of decision making on p 20.

Detailed information on this issue can be found in Taylor, F (1987, 2nd edn) *After School: a Guide to Post School Opportunities*, London: Kogan Page. But a flow chart summary of possibilities as an initial stimulus is given opposite.

Now is the time to be thinking about the possibility of a year between A Levels and the next stage of your life. Universities believe that such a year can, if productively used, provide a valuable experience helping you both to contribute to, and to gain from, your course. Mathematics departments, though, often prefer to take students without the gap.

There are two ways to set something up.

One is to make all the arrangements yourself. You can, for instance, look in *The Lady* for au pair work abroad, or you can write to: CRAC, Hobsons Press, Bateman Street, Cambridge CB2 1LZ for their useful booklet *A Year Off*, which has full details of contacts and leads for all types of activity.

The other way is to use one of the two key organisations which help to place you:

The Project Trust
Breacachadh Castle
Isle of Coll
Argyll
Scotland PA78 6TB;   087 93 444

GAP Activity Projects (GAP) Ltd
7 Kings Road
Reading
Berkshire RG1 3AA;   0734 594914

It is a very good idea to write early to these organisations, say in the summer term of your lower sixth year. For the Project Trust you need to be between 17¼ and 19½ years old inclusive at the

Some main employment and course routes after A Levels

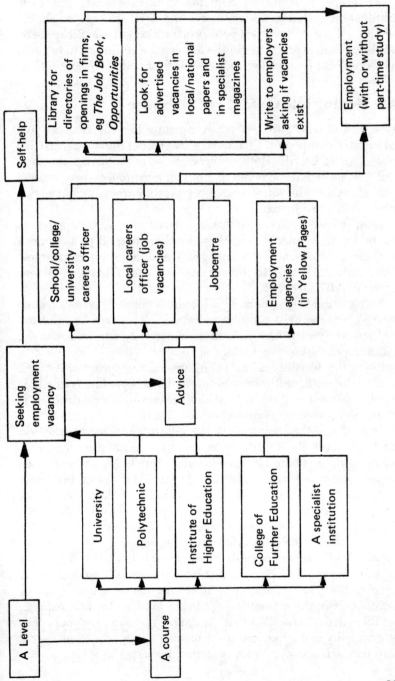

time of going overseas; registration closes at the end of January for those going overseas in September of that year, but early application is strongly advised. For the GAP scheme you should be 18 by the time you start your project; and you should apply by not later than April to begin the following autumn, or to begin in the New Year (you can go for between four and nine months).

9.3 Getting into Oxford or Cambridge

You need to be gifted, a really outstanding student; not just talented or competent. That means, as a rule of thumb, at least five grade As at GCSE. Both universities want to attract as many realistic applicants as possible, but you need to feel there is some special reason why you should apply. As they are only eight weeks' long, terms are intense.

Competition is keen. At Oxford each year, 7,000 applicants apply for 3,000 places; and these applicants tend to have been pre-selected by schools or colleges. Conditional offers are most commonly AAB or ABB: 80 per cent of a year's intake at Oxford achieves ABB or better.

Preparation is best done by widening your A Level work, once your A Levels are smoothly under way. This will be from the spring term onwards of your first year in the sixth form. Do the widening out according to interest.

Enquiries to colleges can begin around the spring of the first year in the sixth, and going to summer term open days is a help. If a college has a number of teaching fellows in your subject, it is strong in it, which may attract or divert you!

Oxford and Cambridge have the reputation to attract the best students, and the resources to set up special procedures for selecting them. Oxford has an entrance exam in November of your upper sixth year (Mode E); it is well regarded if you sit this, and it suits you if you are a subject specialist. You can alternatively seek an offer conditional on the outcome of your A Levels (Mode N); this Mode attracts the good all-rounder. In some subjects at some colleges, one or the other Mode is preferred; and all pre-A Level candidates for Medicine must enter by Mode E. Cambridge uses S Level papers or STEP papers, which are taken along with your A Levels. Both universities will also consider you after your A Levels, but for the year following; there would not be entry papers.

Offers are a 'sensed' or 'felt' business. You can help yourself at interview by being likeable and – most crucially – by 'thinking on your feet'. Hence look again at section 1.5 on p 17.

It is essential for anyone contemplating Oxbridge entry to consult closely with their school or college.

9.4 Choosing university courses and other training

In general, this takes place in the *summer term of the first year* in the sixth form. The autumn term is too late for this work, and in any case there is too much work pressure from your ordinary study.

Choose your degree or vocational course primarily on the basis of *liking*, then look at location. Go first for the course you find most attractive. People drop out because they do not like their course: they lose motivation. Conversely, liking your course means interest, and interest means willing work. The amount of work you do in higher education is more important than being bright. Consider, also, how much tuition you will receive: this varies from university to university. Note, too, the balance between continuous assessment and the final exam, as this too varies. Now consider *location*. Is the university civic (in a city), redbrick (just outside a city) or campus (in the country)? How much accommodation is on and off site? Careful consideration of these points can make all the difference to your happiness.

Be prepared to *write* to institutions, or phone, to find out further information. Universities do not mind this, and often one can obtain useful information. For instance, a phone call to the Chartered Society of Physiotherapy revealed the following levels of difficulty in entry:

Very competitive	Bath
	Cambridge
	Guy's
Averagely competitive	Bristol
	Manchester
	Liverpool
	Wolverhampton
Less competitive	Salford
	Teesside
	Birmingham.

Visit universities and polytechnics. The summer is an excellent time for this.

Ask your teachers what they think you'll achieve at A Level. Then you can apply for the courses and universities which are at the right level for you. It's no use going for Bristol, Exeter, Durham and so on if you are not likely to achieve the grades.

The following tables may help you in your thinking:

A selection of career openings after degrees in the stated subjects

Subject	Career openings include:
Biology	Medical laboratory scientific officer, research, hospital biochemist, teaching, sales, management trainee
Chemistry	Research, product development, quality control, research and development, technical advisory work, teaching
Computer Science	Computer programming, software engineer, software development, systems programmer
Economics	Chartered accountant, financial management, actuary, insurance broking, investment analyst, stockbroking, management trainee
English	Teaching, secretarial, solicitor, journalism, management trainee, police, social work, chartered accountancy, librairianship, publishing
Geography	Teaching, retail management, transport planning, chartered accountancy, librarianship
History	teaching, chartered accountancy, insurance, solicitor, retail management, advertisement sales, estate agent, management trainee
Languages	Teaching, marketing, administration, secretarial
Maths	Teaching, computer programming, software engineer, systems analyst, statistician, systems engineer, chartered accountant, actuary
Music	Teaching, advanced performing, singer, musical director, stage management
Philosophy	Higher degree, solicitor, social work, management, chartered accountant, teaching
Physics	Higher degree, research, research and development

	(R & D), development engineer, engineer, medical physicist, technical advisory work, electronics engineer, quality control, teaching, computer programming, systems engineer, systems analyst
Politics	Chartered accountant, finaancial management, insurance broking, residential social work, social work, child care work, community worker, civil service, housing management, teaching, management trainee, journalism
Psychology	Higher degree, residential social work, social work, child care work, nursing, clinical psychologist, marketing
Sociology	Residential social work, social work, voluntary work, child care work, community work, teaching, retail management, nursing, housing management, police

The changing occupational balance

Expanding occupations	*Contracting occupations*
Production industries	Production industries
Engineers, scientists and technologists	Support services (eg clerical) and personal services
Technicians	Operatives
Multiple-skilled craftsmen	Single-skilled craftsmen
Service industries	Service industries
All professions	Managers, administrators, technicians, craftsmen and operatives
Support services (part time)	Support services (full time)
Personal services (part time)	Personal services (full time)

A most useful book to help you sort out your future career is: Donald, V (1986) *How to Choose a Career*, London: Kogan Page. It covers a good deal of ground in a fresh and easy-to-read style. There is a particularly useful section on careers with good prospects.

9.5 Planning a fall-back

Don't say: 'It's university or nothing!' You may not think this later if your grades are not good enough for university. About half of university applications are unsuccessful. Universities are interested only in high-grade A Level passes: As and Bs, Cs just about, but not Ds or Es.

Polytechnics are still under-rated. There is a tendency for students, parents and employers to regard polytechnic graduates less highly than university graduates. But sometimes polytechnic courses are far better than university courses, and polytechnic lecturers have fewer postgraduate students and fewer research projects of their own, and therefore more time for teaching. There is evidence that students of similar ability achieve better degree results in polytechnics than in universities.

Do not assume it is invariably easy to enter a polytechnic. Polytechnics like Oxford, Bristol, Kingston and Portsmouth are popular. In general, polytechnics in the south and west are harder to get into than those in inner London or in the north and east. Competition for places in law, accountancy and business studies is keen; one polytechnic receives 3,500 applications a year for business studies at degree level, making 600 offers for 70 places (some students drop out, fail or go elsewhere). Business studies degrees typically attract 2,000 applications for 100 places. The easier subjects at polytechnic are subjects like physics, chemistry and engineering.

So, look at courses in polytechnics and in institutes of higher education. During the summer at the end of your first year in the sixth form, you can do some useful work in planning a fall-back. Buy the *Sunday Times, Sunday Telegraph* or *Observer* for all the Sundays in August. You'll see advertisements there from polytechnics and institutes of higher education, which will be filling up their places from the second year sixth formers who have taken A Levels. Note some of the courses advertised: you can apply for them during the autumn term of your second year in the sixth form, as a saver for after A Levels. During the second part of August, *The Times* carries specific polytechnic and university vacancies by course and institution, so pinpointing where applications might be specially welcome when you apply.

Since 1986, the polytechnics have operated a central admissions scheme (PCAS) rather like the universities' system (UCCA). The PCAS scheme applies to all full-time and sandwich first degree, DipHE and HND courses except those in Art and Design and in initial Teacher Training (which will continue to use their respective clearing houses). Courses covered by the existing clearing houses in Social Work and Physiotherapy are not included either, although some institutes of higher education have chosen to join the scheme.

Don't ignore HNDs (Higher National Diplomas). They are virtually degree level, and you can in fact transfer from them to degree courses if you do well. They require a minimum one pass at A Level plus four at GCSE, ie five different subjects in all. A second subject should normally have been studied to A Level, though not necessarily passed. (Two AS Levels would satisfy the one A Level minimum required, and an additional two AS Levels could stand in place of the second A Level normally studied.) On your PCAS form, you might choose to put down two degree course choices and two HND choices (you have four choices in all).

Consider, too, the institutes of higher education outside the PCAS scheme. They run degrees and HNDs. They do not have a central admissions scheme, so you can apply to as many of them as you like.

9.6 Completing a good application form

All applications should ideally be sent off *by half term* of the autumn term in the second year of the sixth. For some application deadlines there will be time in hand, but it is best for you and for the application if it is sent off by half term (main applications and fall-backs too). You can do this providing you have used the summer term of the first year sixth well.

References are crucial. There are:

1. References you write about yourself, ie a personal section which you complete. *Do not* simply say the course is interesting. This tells the admissions tutor nothing. Hundreds of students do this, and it drives admissions tutors mad. *Instead*, reveal yourself: talk about your motives for applying and cite bits of the course that interest you and why; highlight relevant experience and relevant interests; the real you must come through what you write.

2. References that your referee writes on you. Give your referee some information about yourself. This is so simple to do but so often not done. In doing this, you help yourself and you help him. Tell him:

> Why you have chosen this particular course
> Any interests you have which are relevant to the course
> Special skills or abilities you have
> Details of activities you do within your school or college
> Details of activities you do outside your school or college
> Any other interests
> Holiday jobs
> Visits

make a photo copy lic. & write ar answers

Try always to complete application forms in rough first. If *on* you can get hold of two copies of the form, this is best of all. *re* Or you can make a photocopy. Failing that, first fill in the *pa* form using pencil. Watch legibility. *fir*

9.7 Doing well in an interview

This section deals with university and polytechnic interviews, but it is relevant to any interview. The intention is to assemble some notes which you can use beforehand. A good deal of preparatory thinking needs to be done.

Some general preparation   *make a copy of it*

1. Think back over your application form. Is there anything on it that may be brought up as a question in the interview? Is there anything outstanding on your form which would come to an interviewer's attention? High marks in exams, or low marks in exams? An unusual interest?

2. Reflect on your A Level subjects. In what ways are they the same? In what ways are they different? Which do you like best and why? Be ready for some general questions on particular parts of your A Level work. You will have to reflect intellectually.

3. Go to another, not very important interview first if you can. The best way of learning is by experience. If you have had a real-life interview first, this will be a great help to you. Mock interviews are a bloodless substitute: there is no substitute for the real thing.

Working out questions in advance

1. Work out questions they might ask you. One cannot be precise about this, but there are six very popular questions. You should think about them very carefully before the interview.

(a) *Why do you want to go to university?* Well, why do you? If it's because you have a genuine interest in further study, fine. If you think you'll be able to develop as a person there, fine. But going to follow everyone else is not fine. Nor is going because you can't think of anything else to do. Really wanting to study your course is the proper reason for going. The people who drop out of university are people who don't like their courses – they haven't the motivation to go through with them.

(b) *Why do you want to study this course, and not another one?* You must know about your course in detail, and also know about other similar courses.

(c) *Why do you want to come to this particular university?* Well, it may be for the course, but there are other possible reasons, eg location, reputation. Remember, your application must hang together: that is, it must make sense to the interviewer, and everything must be seen to be done for a good reason.

(d) *What do you want to do after your degree?* If your degree course has a logical follow-on to it, this strengthens the reason for accepting you. In reality, though, the powers of analysis and evaluation which a degree course encourages are useful in any job.

(e) *What interests do you have?* There is a tendency to look for students who have some outside interests, to balance their studies. Admissions tutors do not want their faculties full of Jacks made dull by all work and no play. They tend to look for a well rounded personality. Don't be tempted to make up interests, though: it is embarrassing if your shallowness is exposed.

(f) *What do you think about . . . (some item in the news)?* It isn't a bad idea to read a quality newspaper for a week or so before your interview. A reflective and all-round awareness is looked for, and thus you might be asked about a major item in the news.

2. Work out questions you might ask them. It is virtually certain that you will have this chance, and you mustn't pass it by. A

student with no questions comes across as very passive and accepting. Think up some questions to which you really do want an answer. You are going to spend a reasonable portion of your life at university or polytechnic (three or four years), so you ought to have some questions. You can have a specific area in mind to ask about, or you can have specific questions instead, either about the course content or about more varied things as well. Have detailed questions on the course content: it is a good idea. Other questions are important too, such as what previous graduates from your course have done, or how the course is assessed (ie all on the exam, or is some of the final assessment based on course work?).

The day arrives
Two very simple points, so obvious that they shouldn't need mentioning, but so many people don't do them:

1. Dress sensibly and be well groomed.
2. Be on time. No one minds if you're early.

Your mood before the interview
It is important to get this right, and discussion of this time is often omitted.

Talking to the other candidates helps to ease the tension: they are often very nice, and in any case it helps you to know that they are as nervous as you are. But the very fact that you have been invited for interview means that they like the look of you on paper. You are half way there already.

One big point, therefore, is to get yourself into a cheerful mood. They want enthusiasm, but not spilling all over the place: it must be quiet enthusiasm, and directed towards your course, towards particular interests – and towards people in general. You must be cheerful and alive, but not overwhelmingly so, and within the limits of the real you. You have to be able to speak about your good qualities in a positive way, but modestly and without being boastful.

Flowing from this, then, is the second big point: you should try to be thoughtfully and pleasantly assertive in what you say. Have your view. Say it. They want to hear it. And do all this politely and pleasantly. Don't domineer, be dogmatic, rude or dominant, but do say what you think in an amiable way. Maintain this stance even when under attack. Being under attack is no reason to change your view, but if you don't say quite what you mean, you are perfectly at liberty to revise your original statement.

They are looking for nice people whom they'd really rather like to teach.

Stage I of the interview: Defrosting
Say good morning or good afternoon. Give a firm hand-shake (there is a tendency to interpret a limp hand-shake as meaning a wishy-washy person, though that initial impression could be revised in interview). Sit back on the chair, not on the edge.

Stage I is really 'defrosting', and you'll probably be asked insignificant questions such as those about how you travelled to the interview.

Stage II of the interview: They ask you questions
You will notice when the interview 'changes gear': the discussion moves on to more important areas.

They are after the real you, underneath all your learned responses. Give them just that. Say what you really think, and expand on an initial short statement. Don't just grunt a few words in reply. Speak in an honest and frank way. If you don't know the answer to a question, say so. If you say something contradictory, point this out yourself and then try to resolve the contradiction.

Stage III of the interview: You ask them questions
You will have prepared some, as mentioned above. Your questions not only show your interest, but give the interviewer a chance to speak. Interviewers like speaking, and yours will enjoy it if you can encourage him to talk. This will aid your cause.

Stage IV of the interview: Rounding off
You know the end is coming when he says, 'We'll let you know.' This will be after about 20 minutes. End with a smile and a thank-you.

9.8 Waiting for the results

If your exams did not go as well as you were hoping, you can write to universities asking them still to accept you if your grades are a little below your target. Explain your position. Do this before the middle of July. It may help. If there are special factors, your school or college could write on your behalf.

9.9 When the results come out

This section explains the normal course of events, though there may be minor variations from year to year.

HOW TO SUCCEED IN A LEVELS

The universities and polytechnics receive A Level results a little before the Thursday on which they arrive in schools and colleges.

By the Friday, a university department must tell the Admissions Office how many applicants have met their offers and of these, how many are likely to withdraw because the university was their second choice, and they have achieved grades for their first choice university. A list of 'near miss' applicants must be supplied also: those who missed their offer by one or two points (if you are three points down, your chance of keeping your offer is minimal).

On the Monday, the Admissions Committee decides which 'near miss' applicants to accept; on the whole, those who have achieved good grades in the subjects of special relevance to their course will be accepted.

By Tuesday, departments are told which applicants have been accepted, and admissions staff begin to have a clear idea of vacancies. You will now understand why UCCA and the universities ask you to wait for three working days after the issue of results, before ringing universities.

On Wednesday, you can begin ringing round, if you still need a place. Have your UCCA number ready. Ask for Admissions. If there's a course that seems suitable for you, you may be transferred to an Admissions Tutor; be ready to justify yourself. He or she can then ask UCCA for your form. Note that UCCA sends your form to only one university at a time, so don't 'play the field'. About a third of clearing applicants are successful in gaining a university place, and of these, 80 per cent were simply confirming an informal offer made over the phone. Remember that the competition for accountancy, law, and management will be greater than for modern languages, physics, chemistry and engineering.

Expect the ringing-round process to last for several days; and of course include polytechnics too. The places that polytechnic applicants decline, in favour of university, will keep coming on to the market right through September: perhaps 80 per cent of polytechnic applicants have also applied to university. Remember that less popular, or new, courses ask for lower grades.

From the Wednesday onwards, vacancy information is available centrally by phoning UCCA and PCAS: spare places and points required can be given, but not personal advice. Vacancies are available through PRESTEL and also through the Times Network Systems (TTNS). *The Times* itself carries vacancies, and specially keep your eye on the Sunday papers such as the *Observer* or *Sunday Telegraph*, where vacancies are advertised.

Remember the University of Buckingham, which runs degrees in business, the humanities, law and science. Courses start in January. You apply direct (they are outside UCCA). Consider, too, degrees in institutes of higher education. Many of these institutes are outside a central admissions system. Their guide can be obtained from: The Administrative Officer, Standing Conference of Principals, Edge Hill College of Higher Education, Ormskirk, Lancashire L39 4QP.

If you need extra advice, the UCCA clearing panels open at the beginning of September, and you can discuss your case with them. And your local careers office will have a specialist available for a personal interview.

You may feel like appealing against your results. This must be done through your school or college, who must feel there is a serious discrepancy between your actual, and expected, results. Rarely are results changed, and then only after weeks or months. Irrelevance is the most common explanation for a result lower than expected. Remember it is common practice for schools to send in expected grades. Boards check these against actual grades, and check discrepancies; all this will have already been done when you receive your results. If you press ahead with an appeal, take other initiatives in addition.

You may consider re-taking your A Levels, if you feel you can do better and view the prospect positively. The options are: (a) return to school, though this may feel like taking a step backwards; (b) take a correspondence course, where you will need the motivation to work on your own; (c) go to a college of further education locally – their provisions vary; (d) go to a 'crammer'. They are effective but expensive, and tend to be concentrated in London and Oxford. Free information about them can be obtained from: Gabbitas Truman and Thring Educational Trust, 6–8 Sackville Street, Piccadilly, London W1X 2BR.

Remember, too, that if you have passed two A Levels, they can be very useful in the job market. There are good openings in: Government research establishments, computer and software firms, building societies, newly privatised industries, the Civil Service, large retail firms, and administration work in the health service.

Index

applications 57, 98, 105–6
Arts subjects 13–14, 95
AS Levels 95–7
bar charts 86
bias 18
Biology 14, 94–5
browsing 22
Buzan, T 32–6
Cambridge 100
career openings 102–3
Chemistry 14, 94–5
choice of A and AS Levels 92–7
concentration 74
conceptual thinking 19
coursework 81–91
crammers 111
decision making 20
diagrams 31–2
discussion 14–16
empathy 18–19
English Literature 13, 35, 41–4, 48–51, 82
essays 39–44, 69–72
examiners 73
exams 67–73
    marks 70
experiments 90–91
fall-backs 104–5
flow charts 36–7
gap year 98–9
GCSE 16–17, 92–4
Geography 13, 31–3
goal setting 74
grammar 65
graphs 84–5
group discussion 14–16
handwriting 62–3
History 48
holidays 55–60
index cards 47–8
inner speech 25
interest 75
interviews 106–9
issue of results 109–11
learning 77–80
libraries 21–2
maps 31–3
Maths 31, 48–9, 92, 94–5
medicine 93
memory 46, 76–7

modern languages 13, 31, 93
moral thinking 19
motivation 56, 74–5
multiple-choice questions 72
notes 26–31
    alternatives to 31–7
    and see revision
organisation of material 78
Oxford 100
paragraphing 39–44, 71–2
patterns and notes 32–6
Physics 14, 37–8, 94–5
physiotherapy 94, 101
polytechnic 101–5
private study 16
problem solving 20
procrastination 74
rapid reading 23–5
reading skills 22–5
recreation 62
regression 23
reinforcement 79–80
relevance of exam answers 39, 67–9
repetition 78
results 109–11
retakes 111
retroactive inhibition 78
revision 45–51, 52, 55, 57–61, 79
Robinson, F P 80
scanning 22, 27
science 14, 93–5
search skills 21–2
skimming 22–3
sleep 61
spelling 66
spotting 61
SQ3R method 80
stress 62
subvocalisation 25
tables 87
term time 53–4
thinking 17–20, 75–6
time 52–66
underlining 36
university 100–103
vocabulary 31
wide reading 22, 57
    see also notes
written work 54